D1096608

BAZI FRONTIERS

THE COSMIC GEOGRAPHY OF SUCCESS

Dr. Lily Chung & Samantha Lam

PALLADION PRESS

LONDON

Copyright © 2019 Lily Chung and Samantha Lam

First published in 2019 by Palladion Press, an imprint of Palladion Publishing Ltd. All rights reserved. No part of this publication may be reproduced, distributed or transmitted in any form or by any means, electronic or mechanical, including photocopy, recording, or any information storage and retrieval system, without permission in writing from Palladion Publishing, or as expressly permitted by law or under the terms agreed with the appropriate reprographic rights organisation. Enquiries concerning reproduction which may not be covered by the above should be addressed to Palladion Publishing at the address below.

Palladion Publishing Ltd.
20-22 Wenlock Road
London, N1 7GU
United Kingdom

Bazi Frontiers: The Cosmic Geography of Success / Lily Chung and Samantha Lam. - 1st ed.
ISBN 978-1-9993759-1-1 (paperback)

CONTENTS

LIST OF FIGURES

PREFACE

This book is aimed principally at intermediate students of Chinese metaphysics, though it ought to be readable by anyone with a serious interest in the subject, as well as a familiar understanding of the Five Elements and their associated stem-branch interactions.[1] It has sprung from a desire not only to unveil the mysterious face of this classical Chinese cosmology, but also to invigorate it with the spirit of dynamic research, for which we hope every student will take accountability.

The Four Pillars *Bazi* method of divination is an adaptable system, capable of responding to the passage of time, and never static or rigid in its application. Distilled from over a thousand years of empirical insight into the energy flows that preside over time and place, its codification was the collective endeavor of ancient Chinese sages who had been seeking an elaborate answer to the mystery of cosmic inequality.

By interpreting birth data in accordance with the principles of the system they had created, these early metaphysicians were able to provide a roadmap of the cosmic landscape into which we are born, as well as key information allowing us to navigate life via the path of least cosmic resistance. For example, it forecasts a greater incidence of success upon the onset of an auspicious energy flow, while the inverse is also true. The consensus within Bazi circles is that the composition of Five Elements within a chart is key to decoding its destiny, but what constitutes destiny, and who or what governs it?

The Chinese term *mingyun* (命運) has no literal counterpart in English, though it is typically translated as "fate" or "destiny". Taking

---

1 Readers who have grasped the essence of *The Four Pillars of Destiny, Discover Your Code to Success* (Chung & Peh, 2013) should be well-equipped to follow our discussions.

each character on its own merits, *ming*[2] (命) is a "mandate" or "decree", an instruction imposed from above; the character *yun* (運), on the other hand, has more flexible connotations, often understood as "luck", but literally also to "move" or "carry". Taken as a whole, the term encapsulates the tug and pull between that which has been pre-ordained and the influence of one's volition.

The greatest metaphysician of China, Shao Kangjie[3] (born Shao Yong of the Song dynasty, 1011-1077), professed that one's destiny is the work of the Almighty tempered by human variables. In his seminal publication *Huang Ji Jing Shi* (皇極經世), Shao was the first to advance the idea that individuals could successfully alter the course of fate by upgrading the quality of their Bazi with good deeds.

In his view, life was composed of two elements: one part being a gift from God (the cosmic energy, or *qi,* presiding over one's birth), and the other governed by external factors, associated with solo effort and one's immediate environment. He maintained that while we are powerless to choose our own Bazi, we can nevertheless significantly enhance it by carrying out "good works". Conversely, without the commensurate human effort needed to develop a superior grade of Bazi, life would deteriorate to that of a worthless system.

Shao did not define "good works" nor document living examples to support his line of inquiry.[4] Technological limitations during his time meant that the population could not be assessed and cross-referenced en masse, as is possible today, yet our shared global history seems to bear out his foresight.

---

2 Sometimes written as *Meng.*
3 His biography and life chart has been previously discussed in *The Four Pillars of Destiny, Your Life Numbers and Hexagrams from the I Ching* (Chung & Peh, 2015).
4 For further reading on this topic, see *Liao Fan's Four Lessons* (了凡四訓), written by Yuan Liao Fan of the Ming dynasty. The principle that man is capable of changing his fate through good action is well documented in this important discourse. Over the course of four "lessons", the writer provides several examples of good deeds and their impact, as well as those of his contemporaries, concluding that through action, either positive or negative, one ceases to be bound by fate, but holds the key to destiny creation itself.

Our goal is to pay tribute to Shao, completing the work he set forth in his treatise, and furnishing our readers with the data and examples needed to support the timeless statements enshrined in this important work. More than 90 examples have been collected, the result of Lily's determined efforts over several years of biographical study. Many have three or four birth counterparts, all leading different lives. The data should enable us to compare the range of responses from individuals born at a given time, who are subject to interactions forged amid the very same cosmic terrain.

While current literature on the subject does not provide a dependable frame of reference, thanks to having key data at our fingertips in today's digital age, we have been able to assume the mantle of responsibility for conducting the research that eluded Shao Kangjie in his day.

London
November 2018

L.C.
S.L.

CHAPTER ONE

INTRODUCTION

In her decades of experience as a practising Four Pillars metaphysician, Dr. Lily Chung has been able to witness the interplay of cosmic flows manifesting as recurrent success for those with a superior blend of the Five Elements in their cosmic system. One observation, however, remains puzzling: those born on the same exact date are often subject to remarkably divergent destinies. In other words, people with identical birth charts respond in a range of ways to the same prevailing cosmic energy, yielding personal histories that often bear little resemblance to one another.

It is easy to see, for example, how a trio of cosmic flows could result in a sudden windfall, Nobel prize, or Olympic medal. Yet the same trio combination is often also experienced as the more mundane conclusion of a business deal or a marriage alliance. It would appear that an auspicious Bazi does not necessarily guarantee prosperity to all those that own it.

This phenomenon has been troubling metaphysicians since day one, with multiple theories advanced yet none of them conclusive. Many practitioners place convenient blame for the disparity on a time difference of a matter of minutes within the birth hour, data that is typically unavailable in the public record. As a matter of fact, the birth time influence does not figure prominently in the development of our lives until we reach late middle-age. Its significance is minimal unless subject to a process which involves the other pillars in a special configuration. Even the lives of twins, born so close in the hour element, are not immune to the vagaries of individual fate, and their widely variable achievements speak for themselves.

The objective of our investigation is twofold. Firstly, we would like to demonstrate how cosmic flows converge to generate success or failure at a given point in time. The solid evidence we require is taken from personalities who have achieved fame in the modern age through phenomenal successes that best showcase the work of cosmic energy, providing classic textbook illustrations of Bazi in practice. We document their key life events, highlighting the way in which certain goals are achieved upon the concerted interplay of cosmic flows.

Secondly, we seek to illustrate the way in which people born at the same time, with the same presiding birth energies, nevertheless go on to experience very different destinies. For this, we have taken samples of notable individuals, each one having at least one counterpart with a duplicate birthday. We hope that the juxtaposition of their unique stories will provide much-needed insight into the way that external factors, such as one's geographical location, interact with cosmic flows.

Methodology

The techniques for selecting our sampling criteria were twofold. Firstly, they had to be drawn from a pool of top-tier contemporary figures in society, all achieving a notable degree of success within their chosen fields. These included current national leaders, prize-winning scientists, and billionaires from *Forbes*' list of 2015. The billionaires were then narrowed down into the following categories:
- the 50 richest persons worldwide,
- America's richest self-made women,
- China's 100 richest people, and
- Russia's 20 richest people.

Secondly, each sample needed a complete birthday comprising the year, month and day, and at least one notable counterpart with a duplicate Bazi, for the purpose of comparing their key life events.

Why do we pay special attention to Chinese and Russian billionaires? Both of these groups have demonstrated a unique pattern of success that offers new insight into the practice of Bazi. We have assigned an individual chapter to each group.

Of the 96 samples investigated, only 48, along with their counterparts, are discussed in this book. The remainder forms a pool of valuable data to be mined by diligent readers, eager to flex and advance their knowledge of Bazi. The names of these additional 48 samples are listed in the Appendix.

We typically use only three out of the four pillars for each sample due to the difficult task of locating exact birth times in the public record. Some people resort to the Astrological Data Bank, which provides the birth times of various celebrities. We have refrained from doing so in order to avoid the inaccuracies associated with using data outside the public record. In any case, it is best that our samples adhere to a consistent format for the purposes of fair comparison.

An important consideration here is whether the birth hour is crucial in Bazi analysis. Bazi is a marvelously flexible system which, although optimized by the inclusion of all four pillars, generously allows for the use of three pillars without compromising the integrity of the chart. In fact, it is fully acceptable practice (with documented legitimacy) to use three pillars wherever the birth hour is unavailable. As the following chapters demonstrate, our sampled birth composites provide remarkably accurate messages, especially when the other pillars, as well as luck cycle pillars, are used to enhance this insight.

The impact of the hour pillar in one's birth composite normally emerges in our late forties to sixties, depending on the age at which the luck cycles are initiated. Prior to advanced middle-age, the hour pillar may only prove critical for certain systems that, for instance, rely on trios and pairings. The personalities discussed in the following chapters were able to succeed early on in their lives, long before their hour pillars became influential.

Structure

Our book is composed of nine chapters. To facilitate understanding and as a reminder of key principles expounded more fully elsewhere, Chapters Two and Three have been assigned to instruct our readers on the Five Elements concept and basic stem-branch interactions. In the latter, we have added more Bazi formulae which frequently apply to a superior category of chart.

Chapter Four introduces the six most prevalent cosmic systems of the famous or wealthy global elite in order to equip our readers with the background necessary to follow our discussions. Each example has its Bazi type classified and analyzed, with supporting key life events for verification. These discussions set the format and analysis procedure for all subsequent chapters.

Chapters Five and Six consist of case studies on worldwide examples within the same defined parameters. Chapters Seven and Eight follow the case studies of billionaires from China and Russia respectively. Finally, Chapter Nine contains our concluding remarks.

A Note on the Roman Alphabet System used in this book

The adoption of a Roman alphabet system to replace traditional Chinese characters proceeded from Dr. Chung's experiences of teaching Bazi in the 1990s. She soon realized that the traditional Chinese script used to represent stems and branches was wholly unfamiliar to Western audiences, only serving to compound the system's inaccessibility. A natural development was to convert the Chinese perpetual lunar calendar into Roman letters, negating the further step of mastering the 40 or so Chinese characters such calendars contained.[1] This alphabet system began in 1997 following the publication of *The Path to Good Fortune: The Meng* (Chung, 1997), now no longer in print but with a circulation of some 10,000 copies. With both Chung and her students conducting classes using these alphabetized equivalents ever since, it stands to reason that a large number of Bazi students have currently adopted this system in their practice. It is with this in mind that both Roman lettering as well as the traditional Chinese characters have been utilized side by side in the current book. For students who began their journey into metaphysics with other teachers, the traditional characters may already be well memorized. Our book therefore caters to both sets of students and we hope to increase accessibility in this way.

---

1 These converted calendars are attached as appendices to *The Path to Good Fortune: The Meng* (Chung, 1997), currently out of print, and *The Truth of Ups and Downs: Cosmic Inequality* (Chung, 2009).

CHAPTER TWO

MAPPING THE COSMIC ENERGY

THE COSMIC ORDER

When the sages of Chinese antiquity began the task of codifying cosmic energy into the coherent system known today as *Bazi* or Four Pillars, the fabric of our cosmos was perceived as comprising five distinct, yet interdependent, elements. These Five Elements are Wood, Fire, Metal, Water and Earth, each embodying qualities and concepts which collectively form the very building blocks of creation. Understanding the interplay between the Five Elements opens a doorway into the mind of the infinite: the nature of matter from the subtle to the gross, and Man's cosmic dance with the forces governing his navigation through life.

According to cosmic order, each element has its own domain, or sphere of influence (mapped below in figure 2a): Wood resides in the East, Fire in the South, Metal in the West, and Water in the North, while Earth manifests at the centre of all. Similarly, each element takes its turn to rule, waxing and waning with the rotation of the seasons. Wood reigns in springtime, when all vegetation thrives, now in a state of flux after the stillness of winter. With the onset of summer, Fire takes the helm in the form of heat from the sun and lengthening of days. Metal is at its most potent in autumn; it springs from the Earth and undermines it, conquering Wood in the process. Water commands the winters, weakening the Earth, draining the Metal from which it sprang, and extinguishing Fire.

In the final month of each season, the dominating element wanes in power, creating a void filled by rising Earth. Earth thus prevails during the months of lunar March, June, September and December - approximately equivalent to the months of April, July, October and January in the western calendar.

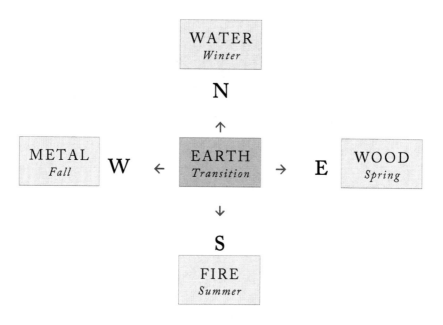

Fig. 2a: Domain of Elements

Each element exhibits both a Yin and a Yang polarity, forming 10 energy variants. Their spatial and temporal distribution is symbolized by 10 Chinese characters called *stems*, signifying their elevation above the ground. The unique attributes of these stems are listed in figure 2b below.

ELEMENT		SYMBOL	PROPERTIES	ATTRIBUTES
丁甲	Yang Wood	Tree, Forest, Lumber	Erect Strong	Kindness Fairness
t乙	Yin Wood	Tree branch, Plants, Shrubs	Gentle Flexible	Kindness Fairness
F丙	Yang Fire	Sun Great heat	Strong Bright, Hot	Courtesy Quickwittedness
f丁	Yin Fire	Man-made fire in all forms	Warm Bright	Warmth Intelligence
E戊	Yang Earth	Massive dry earth, Walls, Mountains	Stable	Reliability Integrity Stability
e己	Yin Earth	Moist earth, Mud supporting vegetation	Moist Metal-empowering	Some integrity
M庚	Yang Metal	Metal ore, Heavy metal, Tools	Uncompromising	Justice Decisiveness
m辛	Yin Metal	Refined metal, Small tools, Jewellery	Shiny Sleek	Polished Delicate
R壬	Yang Water	Rivers, Lakes, Any body of water on ground	Flexible Changeable	Wisdom Creativity Flexibility
r癸	Yin Water	Rain, Drizzle, Snow, Fog Mist, Dew	Flexible Changeable	Elegance Creativity Flexibility

Fig. 2b: Ten Stems

As the energies interact with one another, they transmute in form and strength over time. The 12 earthly *branches* were devised to codify these changes across the span of time, so called due to the fact that they branch from the stems. Collectively, they represent the following categories: the 12 months of the lunar year, the 12 days in a fixed cycle, and the 24 hours in a day divided into 12 pairs (that is, each sign pertaining to a two-hour period). These branches are detailed in figure 2c.

Each stem and branch is represented by a Chinese character. The technical connotations of these characters are normally understood only by those trained in metaphysics. These stem-branches are widely discussed in metaphysical literature, and feature in many other Chinese metaphysical systems such as the popular 12-animal system, which has captured the imagination of amateur practitioners across the world. These animal signs are included in the table for reference, as they have in fact been incorporated into Bazi.

BRANCH	STEM EQUIVALENTS		LUNAR MONTH	DOMAIN	HOURS	ANIMAL
R子	r癸	rain	November *Winter*	North	11pm-1am	Rat
g丑	r癸 e己 m辛	rain earth metal	December *Winter*	Northeast	1-3am	Ox
T寅	T甲 F丙 E戊	trees the sun dry earth	January *Spring*	Northeast	3-5am	Tiger
t卯	t乙	plants	February *Spring*	East	5-7am	Rabbit
W辰	E戊 t乙 r癸	dry earth plants rain	March *Spring*	Southeast	7-9am	Dragon
f巳	E戊 M庚 F丙	dry earth metal ore the sun	April *Summer*	Southeast	9-11am	Snake
F午	f丁 e己	fire mud	May *Summer*	South	11am-1pm	Horse
d未	e己 f丁 t乙	mud fire shrubs	June *Summer*	Southwest	1-3pm	Goat
M申	M庚 R壬	metal ore rivers	July *Fall*	Southwest	3-5pm	Monkey
m酉	m辛	metal	August *Fall*	West	5-7pm	Rooster
H戌	E戊 m辛 f丁	dry earth metal fire	September *Fall*	Northwest	7-9pm	Dog
r亥	R壬 T甲	rivers trees	October *Winter*	Northwest	9-11pm	Pig

Fig. 2c: Branches and their Stem Equivalents

To indicate the changing strength of the elements over time, each stem is matched to a branch. What makes the pairing tricky is the unequal number of signs in each group. In each round of pairings, two signs in the branch group are left without a match. These two signs from the first round become the first two pairing signs in the second round. It therefore takes six stem groups and five branch groups to complete a full cycle. The process is clearly laid out in figure 2d below.

Each stem-branch pair is called a *pillar*. The two signs can be written vertically or horizontally; but in any chosen format, the stem always comes first, that is, on the top or left. Since the pillar represents a manifestation of cosmic energy at a given moment in time, it may also be called a flow pillar, or simply a *flow*.

It takes 60 pillars to complete a full cycle. Each year, month, and day is assigned a pillar as shown in the lunar calendars.[1] The cycle repeats continuously in perpetual order. An identical pillar will appear in a frequency of 60 - that is, 60 years, 60 months (five years) or 60 days (approximately two months). Each pillar tells the climate or flow condition of the year, the month or the day. For example, a Yang Water Rat year (RR壬子) will bring plenty of rain, while a Yang Fire Horse day (FF丙午) occurring in a Yin Fire Snake month (ff丁巳) is likely to be the warmest day in the month. It takes experience, knowledge and skill to interpret these pillars effectively.[2]

---

1 A set of perpetual lunar calendars from 1920-2030 is attached to the appendix of *The Path to Good Fortune: The Meng* (Chung, 1997) and *The Truth of Ups and Downs: Cosmic Inequality* (Chung, 2009).

2 Elaborate discussion of the reading of such pillars may be found in *The Path to Good Fortune: The Meng* (1997).

TR 甲子	tg 乙丑	FT 丙寅	ft 丁卯	EW 戊辰	ef 己巳	MF 庚午	md 辛未	RM 壬申	rm 癸酉
TH 甲戌	tr 乙亥	FR 丙子	fg 丁丑	ET 戊寅	et 己卯	MW 庚辰	mf 辛巳	RF 壬午	rd 癸未
TM 甲申	tm 乙酉	FH 丙戌	fr 丁亥	ER 戊子	eg 己丑	MT 庚寅	mt 辛卯	RW 壬辰	rf 癸巳
TF 甲午	td 乙未	FM 丙申	fm 丁酉	EH 戊戌	er 己亥	MR 庚子	mg 辛丑	RT 壬寅	rt 癸卯
TW 甲辰	tf 乙巳	FF 丙午	fd 丁未	EM 戊申	em 己酉	MH 庚戌	mr 辛亥	RR 壬子	rg 癸丑
TT 甲寅	tt 乙卯	FW 丙辰	ff 丁巳	EF 戊午	ed 己未	MM 庚申	mm 辛酉	RH 壬戌	rr 癸亥

Fig. 2d: Stem and Branch pairing, 60 Pillars

The 24 hours of a day are divided into 12 zones. Each two-hour zone is defined by one of the branches. These zones are listed in figure 2e below.

HOUR	BRANCH		HOUR	BRANCH	
1-3	g丑	Ox	13-15	d未	Goat
3-5	T寅	Tiger	15-17	M申	Monkey
5-7	t卯	Rabbit	17-19	m酉	Rooster
7-9	W辰	Dragon	19-21	H戌	Dog
9-11	f巳	Snake	21-23	r亥	Pig
11-13	F午	Horse	23-1	R子	Rat

Fig. 2e: Hour Zones

Now that we have provided a rudimentary explanation of the cosmic order, it falls on our readers to consult the lunar calendars and test, verify, and account for the cosmic flows.

Origin of the Bazi system

The perpetual lunar calendars of cosmic flows form the fundamental building blocks of Bazi. This system was devised and refined over a lengthy period of about 800 years,[3] the result of a monumental and combined effort by the sages of Chinese antiquity.

It resulted in the Four Pillars divination system, itself consisting of two parts: the birth composite and luck cycle. The birth composite consists of four cosmic flow pillars, one each for the year, month, day and time of one's birth. These are represented by the Five Elements and provide a complete snapshot of the energies prevalent at the time of one's birth to the nearest two-hour window. It describes the Self's cosmic endowments, which subsequently translate into one's abilities, character, physical attributes, opportunities in life and, in short, the entire blueprint for one's earthly existence.

The quality of our birth composite, however, changes periodically, - typically every five years, the block of time accorded to each individual period of the luck cycle. This means that the fundamental energy of our birth composite changes every five years, following the onset of new energy flows from our luck cycle.

While an exceptional birth composite goes hand in hand with an exceptional life, there is no lifetime guarantee. The onset of a detri-

---

3 N.B. This period does not account for the history of the development of the lunar calendars themselves. A brief history of the development of the system of Bazi has been discussed in *The Path to Good Fortune: The Meng* (1997), and *The Truth of Ups and Downs: Cosmic Inequality* (2009).

mental flow could quite suddenly topple this fortune. Yet, with the timely advent of supportive flows from the luck cycle somewhere further down the line, one eventually bounces back. Similarly, an ill-fated birth composite, typically bestowing great misfortune on its bearer, should not necessarily be taken to mean that all is lost - a sudden surge in fortunes could manifest at the onset of a particularly fortunate flow.[4]

Understanding the parameters and workings of one's energy system is key to formulating a strategy for flowing with it. During our peaks, we ought to be making preparations for a soft landing, rather than freefalling in dramatic fashion once the troughs arrive. In the deep valley of our darkest hours, we must shelter our assets from rain, ensuring survival by placing the nose to the grindstone and avoiding senseless vanity projects. Regardless of individual circumstances, we should always keep our spirits up and hopes alive.

READING THE BAZI

Position of the Pillars

For the purposes of reading the Bazi, we will furnish our explanation with the Four-Pillar cosmic system of Wang Chuanfu, a young scientist-billionaire from China.[5] He was born on February 15, 1966, between 7 and 8 in the evening. This is his birth composite and luck cycle:

---

4 The complete procedure of calculating the birth composite and luck cycle has been explained at length in *The Truth of Ups and Downs: Cosmic Inequality (2009)*, so will not be repeated here. Newcomers to the subject are encouraged to refer to this and aforementioned publications for their further understanding.
5 A more elaborate analysis of this chart can be found in Chapter Seven (p.174).

H	D	M	Y
F丙	t乙	M庚	F丙
H戌	f巳	T寅	F午

	6	16	26	36	46	56
LUCK CYCLE	m辛	R壬	r癸	T甲	t乙	F丙
	t卯	W辰	f巳	F午	d未	M申

The Bazi stands for a complete cycle of 60 cosmic years. Each pillar governs about 15 years of our life, starting from the beginning of the luck cycle period. The year pillar represents the influence of our grandparents, ancestors, and partially, in some cases, our parents as well. Its energy mostly affects the first quarter of our lives. The age of initiation of the luck pillars matters; it becomes the starting age for the period.

As there are two characters per pillar, the stem governs the first 7.5 years of the quarter, while the branch governs the next, making about 15 years in total for each pillar. In our example, the stem (F丙) in Wang's year pillar governs his life from age six to 13.5, while the influence from the branch (F午) commences from age 13.5 to 21.

The month pillar represents parents and, variably, older brothers or relatives. While its effects become more significant in early midlife, its influence upon the Self is lifelong. The month branch is the key to determining the strength of the other signs in the birth composite. For example, a Wood Self, born in the spring months of Tiger (T寅) or Rabbit (t卯), will have been born at the ideal time, enjoying the vigorous mental and physical health this entails; other Wood signs in the birth composite will have similiar strength.

The day pillar officially represents the third quarter of one's life. However, like the month branch, its effects on the Self do not decline with the passage of time. Its branch represents both the health and the spouse palace of the Self, determining quality of marriage and the benefits offered by one's spouse, as well as general well-being.

The hour pillar is the weakest of all four pillars, mainly introducing its effects towards the last quarter of one's life. It indicates the quality of our children and the help we are likely to receive from friends.

Overall, the dividing lines between the pillars are not intended to be well-defined; as with the luck pillars, there is a transitional zone between every period.

To see how the other seven signs of the Bazi relate to the Self, we first need to explain how the elements relate to one another. There are numerous types of interaction but we will concentrate on the two basic ways in which the Five Elements interact (figures 2f and 2g).

Interactions

The Breeding Cycle

The Five Elements support or empower one another in the following manner:

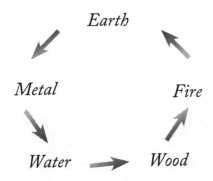

Fig. 2f: The Cycle of Birth or Breeding Cycle

Here, Water makes the Wood grow; Wood fuels Fire; Fire hardens and produces Earth; Earth provides a home for the formation of Metal, while Metal generates Water.

The Ruling Cycle
The Five Elements control one another in the following manner:

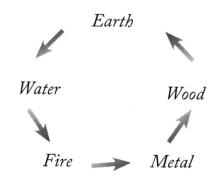

Fig. 2g: Cycle of Destruction or Ruling Cycle

In the process, Water extinguishes Fire; Fire melts down the Metal; Metal chops down the Wood; Wood pierces the Earth; and Earth absorbs or blocks the flow the Water.

In the birth composite, the Self is key to determining how the Five Elements interact. What rules the Self element becomes its *Ruler*. For example, the Ruler of Wang's plant Self, the Yin Wood (t乙), is Metal - Yang Metal to be specific. The Ruler controls and disciplines, refining and impelling its subject to behave. A powerful Ruler creates a Self with a propensity for hard work - indeed, many scholars have strong Rulers in their birth composite. Wang has his Ruler - the Yang Metal (M庚) - standing close by in the month stem, producing a studious individual with an enduring work ethic.

With time, the Ruler came to represent the career star for both sexes. As women were seen as male property in the societal conventions of early China, the Ruler also signified a woman's spouse element. A woman with a powerful and beneficial Ruler or Rulers has great potential towards acquiring a supportive husband (provided the Self is not too weak). For men, a strong Ruler is also a prerequisite for a good career. These are just a few simplified principles.

Signs of the same element of the Self become the *Kin* or *Siblings*. Siblings either support or fight with the Self, and most likely will take on both roles at various times. This principle is exemplified by the Sibling profile of Wang's Bazi. He was born to poor farming parents, both of whom he lost as a young boy. From then on, he grew up under the care of older siblings, who doted on him as though he were their own son. Referring back to his birth composite above, we can see that there are no Sibling elements in his Bazi. Thus, although he has several siblings in reality, none of them treated him as a Sibling rival.

The element the Self controls becomes its *Wealth*. In Wang's case, Yin Wood (t乙) controls Earth. There are four Earth money signs hidden within the four branches and no other Wood signs competing for it. Wang has the potential to become very wealthy, and indeed has become a billionaire with relative ease. The Wealth sign is a tricky customer; just as money itself has a powerful potential to create a great many blessings, so may it also breed evil and harm. Sometimes, a strong Wealth sign could be deadly when there are too many Siblings competing for it.

The element that empowers the Self becomes its *Grantor*, representing the love and devotion received from parents. For Wang's Yin Wood Self, this Grantor is Water. The complete absence of Water in his chart is interesting in that it sets the scene for the premature loss of parental care.

The element that the Self supports is its *Offspring*, figuratively representing children. It governs the aptitude for expression or communication. For the female, it also governs her potential for viable pregnancy or bearing successful children.

Fire is the Offspring of Wang's Yin Wood Self. It is the Yang Fire (F丙) and Yin Fire (f丁) shown in the year and hour stems and hidden in all four branches. He has plenty of it, generating great productivity. Globally, he is one of the largest manufacturer of batteries (Fire).

Depending on the nature of the Self sign, the elements for each category of interaction are different.

For ease of reference, they are summarized in figure 2h below.

		STEMS				
		T甲·t乙 *Wood*	F丙·f丁 *Fire*	E戊·e己 *Earth*	M庚·m辛 *Metal*	R壬·r癸 *Water*
S E L F	T甲·t乙 *Wood*	Sibling	Offspring	Wealth	Ruler	Grantor
	F丙·f丁 *Fire*	Grantor	Sibling	Offspring	Wealth	Ruler
	E戊·e己 *Earth*	Ruler	Grantor	Sibling	Offspring	Wealth
	M庚·m辛 *Metal*	Wealth	Ruler	Grantor	Sibling	Offspring
	R壬·r癸 *Water*	Offspring	Wealth	Ruler	Grantor	Sibling

Fig. 2h: The Interrelation between the Five Elements

CHAPTER THREE

ELEMENTAL INTERACTIONS

The following chapter deals with the fundamental rules governing stem and branch interactions.

STEM INTERACTIONS

Stem Pairings

When used to represent the 10 Selves (or *Day Masters*), the stems may be grouped into five pairs as indicators of harmony and compatibility between signs. Each pair consists of one Yang and one Yin element, illustrated in figure 3a below.

T甲	M庚	F丙	R壬	E戊
Yang Wood	Yang Metal	Yang Fire	Yang Water	Yang Earth
+	+	+	+	+
Yin Earth	Yin Wood	Yin Metal	Yin Fire	Yin Water
e己	t乙	m辛	f丁	r癸

Fig. 3a: The Five Harmonious Stem Pairs

These harmonious stem pairs are applicable to every kind of relationship for gauging its quality and longevity. There will be a heightened degree of compatibility between a Yang Wood Self (T甲) and a

Yin Earth Self (e己), for example, in any social, marital, familial, or commercial field. While minor conflicts may arise now and again, two Selves forming a harmonious pair are intrinsically compatible and, in extreme cases, capable of creating exponentially profitable conditions. Although there may be no guarantee of great fortune, peace generally prevails.

In practical terms, any relationship involving pairing Selves will experience enhancement to the area of life affected by it. For example, a boss-employee pairing could profit the careers of both parties; a parent-child pairing could signify an easier parenting relationship, with the child enjoying a winning edge over his siblings. Pairing Selves tend to forge great friendships as well.

In financial matters, when a Yang Wood Self possesses a Yin Earth in the month or hour stem, the Self is likely to succeed quite phenomenally in financial matters. This pairing process is akin to money pouring automatically into the pockets of the Yang Wood, resulting in easy financial gains as embodied in the Bazi code, *Money seeking the Self*. The analogy applies in the same way to the other four pairs.

BRANCH INTERACTIONS

As indicators of relationship, branches offer more clues than the stems. At any given point, the branches in the year flow, luck cycle, and birth composite will interact with one other, activating a variety of processes.

Branch Pairing

The 12 branches can be divided into six harmonious branch pairs that are indicative of good relationship. Each branch pair consists of one Yang sign and one Yin (figure 3b). Pairing branches in the birth composite indicate good interpersonal and social skills, a person that relates well with others.

In the year and month position, the Self will relate well to parents and older relatives; in the month and spouse position, the Self relates well to the spouse, with the couple working closely towards a common goal; in the hour and day position, the Self relates well to children and friends.

R子	T寅	W辰	F午	M申	H戌
Rat	Tiger	Dragon	Horse	Monkey	Dog
↕	↕	↕	↕	↕	↕
Ox	Pig	Rooster	Goat	Snake	Rabbit
g丑	r亥	m酉	d未	f巳	t卯
EARTH	WOOD	METAL	FIRE	WATER	FIRE

Fig. 3b: Branch Pairing

When a pairing occurs between a sign in the year flow and one in the birth chart, the Self can expect fortunate developments in that particular year, such as marriage, promotion, or success of any kind.

The Trio

The trio is the most powerful indicator of fortune and good relationship of all the combinations discussed so far. A trio is formed by the division of the 12 branches into four groups, each set of three signs comprising either a *directional* trio, or a *harmonious* trio. The directional trio is so named due to its sign groupings belonging to a specific point of the compass (figure 3c). The Pig, Rat and Ox, for example, form a directional trio of the north. In figure 3d, a harmonious trio is formed between every fourth branch in a cycle, for example the Rat, Monkey and Dragon.

A trio derives its power from the merging of all its signs into a single element, which then functions as one united and concentrated form of energy. If the trio happens to be the Self's favored element, tremendous luck can be expected. A complete (and positive) trio in the birth composite produces a well-regarded, well-loved individual, who is able to relate well with others on any level, offering the greatest likelihood of success. A trio also develops when branches from the luck cycle or cosmic year join with a branch or branches in the birth composite, conveying great fortune at the point of convergence. This may take the form of a strong marriage, victory in competition or indeed any kind of successful development.

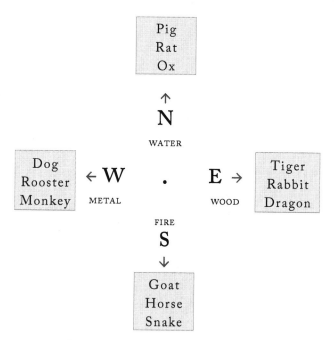

Fig. 3c: The Directional Branch Trinities

WATER	FIRE	WOOD	METAL
M申 Monkey	T寅 Tiger	r亥 Pig	f巳 Snake
+	+	+	+
R子 Rat	F午 Horse	t卯 Rabbit	m酉 Rooster
+	+	+	+
W辰 Dragon	H戌 Dog	d未 Goat	g丑 Ox

Fig. 3d: The Harmonious Branch Trinities

Two of three branches in a trio can form a partial trio, known as an *alliance*. For example, in the Water trio of MRW申子辰, there are three possible Water alliances: MR申子, MW申辰, and RW子辰. Although also an indicator of good fortune, an alliance is a less powerful derivation of the full trio. The same principle applies to the other trio and alliance combinations.

Branches Clashing

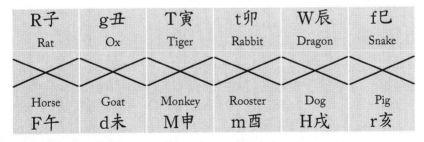

Fig. 3e: Branch Clashing Pairs

There are six clashing pairs, the signs of which are both either Yin or Yang in polarity. Clashing signs indicate instability and disruption in life and relationships. When these clashes occur twice or more in the birth composite, a turbulent life could be the result.

A Self with clashing signs on the year and month branches relates poorly or loosely with one's immediate family. Since these signs are in the first two quarters of the chart, it may also be an indication of unstable family relations in early life. In such scenarios, the Self is always better off preserving a distance from the immediate family.

Clashing branches in the month and spouse position could indicate instability in marriage, but the message is not as strong, and does not cause great concern for the marriage. Clashing branches in the day and hour positions indicate either conflicts with or separation from children - it would be better for the parents to stay away from children during their adulthood.

The onset of a clashing branch from the year flow or luck cycle to one's birth chart is a reliable indicator of disruptions or change at that point in life. Depending on the position at which the clash occurs, and the nature of the branches, each clash presents a different message.

SPECIAL STARS

Each of the 22 signs carry special messages known as stars. The origins of their design are a mystery, yet over time, the information they hold has been invariably accurate.

These stars have been discussed with live examples in previous publications.[1] In this book, we include most of them in reference tables without the accompanying examples. Three separate indicators from our birth composite will allow us to locate the special stars. These are the year branch, month branch and day (or Self) stem.

---

1 The system of stars has been considered in publications such as *The Truth of Ups and Downs: Cosmic Inequality* (2009), *Easy Ways to Harmony* (1999), and elaborated in *Four Pillars of Destiny, Discover your Code to Success* (2013).

Stars by Year Branch

Using the year branch as a reference point, we have chosen three commonly used stars among the group (figure 3d). These are the *Talent* star, *Romance* star (or *Peach Blossom*), and *Mobility* star. Those born in a Rat year, for example, will have the Dragon as their Talent star, the Rooster as their Romance star, and the Tiger as their Mobility star.

Stars of Talent, Romance and Mobility can be located by using the day branch as well. Technically, therefore, we have the potential to possess two stars in each category.

		STAR		
		Talent	Romance	Mobility
	R子	W辰	m酉	T寅
	g丑	g丑	F午	r亥
Y E A R	T寅	H戌	t卯	M申
	t卯	d未	R子	f巳
	W辰	W辰	m酉	T寅
B R A N C H	f巳	g丑	F午	r亥
	F午	H戌	t卯	M申
	d未	d未	R子	f巳
	M申	W辰	m酉	T寅
	m酉	g丑	F午	r亥
	H戌	H戌	t卯	M申
	r亥	d未	R子	f巳

Fig. 3f: Stars by Year Branch[2]

---

2 Note that all the stars in this table are branches.

For the impact of these stars to manifest in life, they have to be present in either the birth composite (four pillars) or luck pillars. In the birth composite, the impact will be lifelong; in the luck pillar, for a period of five years. A useful exercise would be to highlight any potential stars in the branches of both the birth composite and luck pillars for personal reference.

Let us provide a brief synopsis of each star:

Talent (華蓋) denotes outstanding skill in all fields. Successful scholars, scientists, writers, artists, chefs, and designers, for example, are all endowed with special talent. A powerful Talent star usually confers high position on its bearer.

A Romance star creates a well-liked individual that is attractive, charismatic, sociable, generous, and intelligent. As a consequence, it is easier for Selves possessing a Romance star to attract romantic partners, as well as an audience to increase visibility and build fame. The star is crucial for movie stars, singers, writers, and those working in personal relations.

The Mobility star implies travel or change, either physical or mental. People possessing this star in their birth composite are likely to experience varying degrees of mobility in their lives, depending on where the star falls. In the year pillar, the Self is more mobile in the first quarter of life; where it falls in the month pillar, they tend to be more mobile in the second quarter, and so on.

Stars by Month Branch

Several stars can be located using the birth month branch as a reference point. We will focus, however, on just one: the Guard.

The Guard is a great protector, preserving us from evil and danger, stronger and more reliable than the power exerted by the Scholar star discussed further on in this chapter. Practically all great military generals have used it in order to survive on the battle field. Eisenhower had the Guard star combining both Yin and Yang forces into one sign. Many figures of great historical significance have possessed this star, amongst them Isaac Newton, Thomas Edison, Albert Einstein, Richard Nixon and Margaret Thatcher to name a few. In 1984, Thatcher herself escaped a bomb blast in her hotel by the timing of seconds.

MONTH BRANCH	GUARD
R子	R壬 · f巳*
g丑	M庚
T寅	F丙 · f丁
t卯	T甲
W辰	R壬
f巳	M庚 · m辛
F午	F丙 · r亥*
d未	T甲
M申	R壬 · r癸
m酉	M庚 · T寅*
H戌	F丙
r亥	T甲 · t乙

Fig. 3g: Stars by Month Branch

In the table, stars with an asterisk (*) beside it are branches; all others are stems. The two Guard signs for the month represent the dual forces of Yin and Yang. When the Guard star manifests as a single sign, as per the months of Ox (g丑), Rabbit (t卯), Dragon (W 辰), Dog (H戌) and Goat (d未), the forces of Yin and Yang are united in a single entity and its power is intensified. People with this star are wonderful friends to have - helpful and reliable.

Stars by Self

There are 10 Selves represented by stems. Using each Self as a reference point, we have listed three stars in figure 3g, all of which are comprised of branches.

		STAR		
		Scholar	Wealth	Mentor (guide, nobleman)
S E L F S T E M	T甲	f巳・r亥	R子・g丑	g丑・d未
	t乙	F午	g丑・M申	R子・M申
	F丙	T寅・M申	T寅・W辰	r亥・m酉
	f丁	m酉	T寅・W辰	r亥・m酉
	E戊	T寅・M申	R子・g丑	g丑・d未
	e己	m酉	g丑・M申	R子・M申
	M庚	f巳・r亥	R子・g丑	g丑・d未
	m辛	R子	r亥・d未	T寅・F午
	R壬	T寅・M申	M申・H戌	f巳・t卯
	r癸	t卯	M申・H戌	t卯

Fig. 3h: Stars by Self Stem

Those possessing a Scholar Star may be learned and cultivated, or enjoy artistic and literary pursuits. A Scholar star also protects its bearer from evils and danger. Artists, writers and movie stars tend to have prominent Scholar stars.

The Wealth star is typically associated with fame and riches. It takes two branches to make a star. To qualify, the two branches must either be found together in the birth chart, or a combination of birth chart and luck cycle/year flow. In the latter case, prosperity occurs only at that particular point in the person's life.

The Mentor (Guide or Nobleman) functions like an invisible hand, guiding us towards fortune. Having this star in our system is a considerable blessing: the bearer will enjoy an unobstructed and easy path to success. The blessing given depends on the strength of the sign.

SPECIAL PILLARS

Each of the 60 pillars carry special information. Were we to cover the messages of every pillar, there would be enough material to fill a second book. Here, we will expound on a few of these, the effects of which apply to most successful people.

Strategically Intelligent

ER戊子 Yang Earth Rat | mf辛巳 Yin Metal Snake

Selves with one of these pillars will excel in their studies as well as in the management of people. They are intelligent, wise and open-minded.

Intelligent Six

ER戊子 Yang Earth Rat | EF戊午 Yang Earth Horse
eg己丑 Yin Earth Ox | ed己未 Yin Earth Goat
fd丁未 Yin Fire Goat | FF丙午 Yang Fire Horse

A Self which falls into one of these six pillars has a penetrating mind, well-versed in logic and truth; they are all fast learners.

Smart Ten

TW 甲辰	Yang Wood Dragon	MH 庚戌	Yang Metal Dog
FW 丙辰	Yang Fire Dragon	MT 庚寅	Yang Metal Tiger
rd 癸未	Yin Water Goat	RT 壬寅	Yang Water Tiger
mr 辛未	Yin Metal Goat	fm 丁酉	Yin Fire Rooster
tr 乙亥	Yin Wood Goat	EF 戊午	Yang Earth Horse

These Selves are typically quick-witted and intelligent.

Promotional Pillars

TR 甲子	Yang Wood Rat	TF 甲午	Yang Wood Horse
et 己卯	Yin Earth Rabbit	em 己酉	Yin Earth Rooster

A Promotional pillar encourages swift and easy progress in any undertaking. Those falling into this category tend to be accomplished, meeting no impediments upon the road to success. It is best found in the month and day due to the lifelong impact of these pillars. In the hour position, its influence extends from the final quarter of our lives. In the year pillar, its benefits will gradually fade in middle age.

Red-light Pillars

FT 丙寅	Yang Fire Tiger	td 乙未	Yin Wood Goat
TF 甲午	Yang Wood Horse	fd 丁未	Yin Fire Goat
TH 甲戌	Yang Wood Dog	rd 癸未	Yin Water Goat
MH 庚戌	Yang Metal Dog	md 辛未	Yin Metal Goat

Red-light pillars represent problematic interpersonal relationships which, in extreme cases, may cause harm to one's romantic life. Their effect is greatest when present in the day pillar. The worst scenario takes place when both partners in a relationship possess the same Red-light pillar.

CHAPTER FOUR

SUPERIOR TYPES OF BAZI

Bazi types abound in Chinese metaphysics, although no more than a dozen may be found in common usage. Several of these are discussed in *Four Pillars of Destiny, Discover your Code to Success* (Chung & Peh, 2013), and shall not be expounded again here. However, in order to furnish our readers with the theoretical context behind this work, we will cover six special types commonly shared by the individuals whose case histories form the focus of our study. The essential qualities of each will be succinctly described.

These special chart configurations fall into three categories, namely the Variable, the Dominant, and the Follow. Among the three, the Variable is perhaps the most unfamiliar to our Western readers. In classical Bazi literature, it may literally be translated as *Follow the Dominant* - that is, the configuration of the Bazi merges into another type upon the onset of new flows from either the cosmos or the luck cycles. The term "variable" is therefore a more fitting interpretation of the classical Chinese concept, encapsulating its dynamic and somewhat mercurial nature. This precise translation of terms is of high value to non-Chinese speaking readers as it will help to clarify ideas and advance abstract thinking in metaphysics.

Those individuals whose Bazi conform to the Variable configuration thrive on the changeability of useful elements, reacting opportunely and effectively to new circumstances or challenges. The success of their chosen ventures can be swift and staggering, spearheaded as they are by individuals with unique powers of adaptability and resilience in the face of shifting resources. In recent decades, Variable type destinies have been emerging as the most phenomenal among those belonging to the club of the young New Rich. This emergence has become increasingly evident in our research on the high-achieving new billionaires of China and Russia, as well as a substantial number of extraordinarily successful young entrepreneurs worldwide.

Historically, such a system was never highly prized: the Chinese would have considered the bearer unfortunate in having to contend with constant fluctuations of fate and fortune. These early Chinese societies favored conservatism, tending to shy away from radical change or challenges, while valuing instead the peace, stability and comfort that came with cosmic predictability.

Table 4a below classifies our 96 case samples into their respective Bazi configurations (excluding individuals born on the same day). Note that Follow types are further designated into the four sub-groups of Children, Power, Resource and Wealth.

BAZI TYPE		NUMBER	PERCENTAGE
Variable		43	44.8
Follow	Children	6	
	Power	10	
	Resource	10	39	40.6
	Wealth	13	
Dominant		9	9.4
Other		5	5.2
TOTAL		96	100

Fig. 4a: Energy Systems of Case Samples by Number and Percentage

These 96 notable persons comprise 18 national leaders, seven scientists, 14 powerful women and 57 billionaires.[1] According to our body of research into Bazi codes, the highest degrees of success are often associated with the Variable configuration. This is followed by the Follow type, and finally the Dominant. Indeed, our research seems to be revealing an interesting phenomenon, in which subjects belonging to any of these three Bazi types are often significant players in the arena of intense global competition. As shown in Table 4a, a striking 95 per cent of all those sampled can be accounted for by three of the main Bazi types, with 45 per cent of unrelated cases falling within the Variable classification. This suggests that individuals born with one of these auspicious Bazi systems will typically be a notch or two above the rest in their ability to harness great fortune and success.

The following sections will present the essential qualities of the Dominant, Follow, and Variable types - the three main Bazi classification types at the heart of our inquiry. Each of these classifications will be exemplified with a real-world case study of a notable person. The method of analysis used in this book consists of verifying an individual's case history with his or her Bazi pillars and luck cycles. In other words, we have adopted an empirical approach to destiny analysis, based on the concept that our destiny is not randomized, but evolves in ways which have been codified in Bazi theory, a powerful tool to explain why certain events happen at significant junctures in our lives.

§

---

1 Particulars of the 48 case samples not discussed in this book can be found in the Appendix.

DOMINANT

When the Self of a Bazi chart has an alliance or trio that matches its own element, it becomes a Dominant Self. For instance, if a Wood Self (T甲 or t乙) has any two or all of the trio r亥/t卯/d未 in his or her Bazi, he or she becomes Dominant Wood. Similarly, a Metal Self (M庚 or m辛) who has any two or all of the trio m酉/g丑/f巳, will be classified as Dominant Metal. Readers may refer to Chapter Two and Three for elaborations on the other trio combinations.

The formation of a partial alliance or a full trio is an extremely focused and powerful form of energy. Symbolically, it can be likened to that of an army under the charge of the Self as a great general. Given the support of such powerful energies, these individuals are born leaders: confident, dynamic, hard-working, strategic, goal-oriented, and motivated to strive for excellence. Naturally, they tend to excel in their jobs and enjoy great success in life. Our first case study is Hassan Sheikh Mohamud, who was the President of Somalia from September 2012 to February 2017.

HASSAN SHEIKH MOHAMUD
B. NOVEMBER 29, 1955 (JALALAQSI, SOMALIA)

Mohamud is a Somali politician and former President of Somalia, who earned an undergraduate diploma in Technology from Somali National University in 1981, going on to receive a master's degree in Technical Education in 1988 from Bhopal University (now Barkatullah University, India).

He was born in Jalalaqsi, a small agricultural town in central Somalia, where the semi-arid conditions are not particularly conducive to the flourishing of local flora. Considered a steppe climate, its average annual temperature is 28.5 °C while an annual rainfall of just 374 millimeters restricts the full development of trees and plants.

H	D	M	Y
n/a	T甲	f丁	t乙
n/a	F午	r亥	d未

BAZI SYSTEM · DOMINANT WOOD

	17	27	37	47	57
LUCK CYCLE	t乙	T甲	r癸	R壬	m辛
	m酉	M申	d未	F午	f巳

Nevertheless, as a Yang Wood Self, born in a cycle of prime growth, Mohamud is also supported by a Wood team (r亥/d未). This qualifies him as Dominant Wood, a born leader. Additional Wood signs would empower him, with the Rabbit (t卯) as the most auspicious, as it draws his partial Wood alliance into a full trio, the most powerful of Wood flows. The greatest limitation of this Bazi is insufficient Water, a handicap which is correspondingly borne out by the geographical conditions of his birthplace. Sunlight, the output of Wood, would provide an outlet for fame and expression - in figurative terms, illuminating the leaves of the tree and making them shine. His most favorable elements are therefore Wood, Water, and some degree of Fire, with the most harmful element being substantial Metal.

Below are his key life events to support these foregoing considerations.

YEAR	AGE	LUCK CYCLE	KEY EVENTS
1981-85	26-30	Yang Wood, T甲	Teacher in Somalia
1986	31	Yang Wood, T甲	Joined Technical Teachers' Training College in 1984, becoming its department head in 1986
1993-95	38-40	Yin Water, r癸	Education Officer for UNICEF in Somalia
1996-99	41-44	Goat, d未	Consultant on various UN bureaus and development projects
1999-2010	44-55	Goat, d未	Co-established the SIMAD University, becoming its acting dean
2011	56	Rabbit, t卯	Chairman of Peace and Development Party (PDP)
2012	57	Yin Metal, m辛	President of Somalia
2013	58	Yin Metal, m辛	Named in *TIME* as one of the 100 most influential people worldwide

As a Dominant Self, he needs to work hard for a better life. This is particularly evident during his Rooster (Metal) period. In 1986 (FT丙寅), a year of powerful solar energy, he became the department head of the Teachers' Training College at age 31. The timely advent of additional Wood and sunlight played a beautiful duet, elevating him to a position of authority.

During the 1990s, in his Yin Water Goat luck cycle (rd癸未), he was promoted to Consultant and Regional Education Officer of the country. Rain (r癸) set in to bolster his Wood flow while the Goat (d 未) empowered the existing Wood alliance.

In 1999 (et己卯), a Rabbit year, when the Rabbit upgraded his Wood alliance into a trio, he co-established the Somali Institute of Management and Administration (SIMAD) in the capital. The institution subsequently grew into the SIMAD University, with Mohamud acting as Dean until 2010.

In 2012 (RW壬辰), a powerful and watery year, he became President of the country. In the following Yin Water Snake year (rf 癸巳), again characterized by rain, Mohamud was numbered among *TIME* magazine's annual list of the 100 most influential people in the world. He entered a Yin Metal period during his presidency, burdened by the stressful administration.

This example shows how a Dominant Self behaves and how his luck glides with the changing flows. How do others born on the same day experience this destiny? We have two examples.

The first is **Robert James Jeffress Jr.**, an American pastor, best-selling author, and radio and television host. His daily radio show Pathway to Victory, which is broadcast on more than 1,200 television stations in the United States and 28 other countries, can be heard on 764 stations.

As a Dominant Wood Self, he similarly became a leader in his field, albeit spiritual rather than political. He also holds a number of academic degrees, including a Doctorate of Ministry from a Theological Seminary in Texas. In 2006 (FH丙戌), a year of powerful sunshine, Jeffress was awarded the Daniel Award from Vision America, while the Wood year of 2007 saw him elected Pastor of First Baptist church in Dallas, Texas, with a membership of some 13,000 as of 2018. He was courageously outspoken on a range of critical social issues from 2010 to 2012, a period matching Mohamud's action timeline for taking charge of the country.

Meanwhile, **C. David Johnson**, a Canadian actor, has had a career trajectory with less momentum. Although a household name for some time due to his on-screen presence in a long-standing television series, there is overall far less visibility upon the world stage than has been true of his two counterparts.

What created the varying degrees of accomplishment in their careers? The output element as a conduit of fame seems to have been a critical ingredient. Both Mohamud, being born and raised in an agricultural town of a hot country, and Jeffress, raised in tropical Fort Worth, conducting his work primarily from his base in Texas, certainly capitalized on environmental support. In contrast, C. David Johnson, born in the cold and moist climate of Quebec, Canada, is deprived of the warmth and sunlight needed to make his Wood Self shine.

FOLLOW

A Follow type is the opposite of the Dominant Self. The Self in this scenario is feeble; it depends upon a "dominant" element in the Bazi for protection and provision. This dominant element, with its intensely focused energy, becomes its leader, directing its life. The Self submits entirely to the dominant flow.

As a rule, a powerful, solid boss is generous, while at the other end of the spectrum, a weak or shaky boss may be prone to meanness. Wherever they may be found along this spectrum, each boss will demand absolute loyalty from its subject, and a powerful boss will be all the more stringent. For example, a Water Self depending on a Wood flow for its livelihood ought to be standing alone, free of any companion elements in the Bazi that might either vie with the Self for provision or rally the Self to rebellion. To take this a step further, the Self should also ideally be stripped of any supporting Metal elements which may have the unwanted effect of empowering Water and challenging the dominant flow of Wood.

But more importantly, the Self should never "anger" its boss. To illustrate, take a Water sign surrendering to Earth as its provider: such a Self going into a Water cycle would incur very bad luck. Why? Figuratively speaking, one would be trying to build up the strength needed to rebel. The boss, feeling threatened, "punishes" the Self with bad luck, such as carrying out hard work with little or no reward, financial loss, illness, demotion, troubled relationships, and so on. Conversely, a Water Self, entering an Earth luck cycle, would be abundantly rewarded: it would be tantamount to bringing in troops to empower one's boss.

Consequently, those possessing a Follow type Bazi system have a plethora of desirable qualities. The ultimate people pleaser, they tend to be attractive, smart, attentive, considerate and intuitive with a gentle disposition. Such virtues ensure that the Self is handsomely rewarded for its loyalty and subservience. Intuition, in particular, furnishes these individuals with the diplomacy and foresight required to appease or satisfy a powerful commander. Those adhering to a Follow system tend to succeed easily and phenomenally, propelled as they are by an external energy. On the other hand, those with more "regular" systems are sustained only by means of their own limited energy, and move slowly without ever going very far, consequently producing a very ordinary type of success.

Selves with a Follow configuration rarely make mistakes, as they act in alignment with a very concentrated and penetrating energy. Once along the path to success, they also tend to gain riches quickly and abundantly. The reason? Symbolically, their reward comes from the good will of the boss in the form of a lump sum payment, unlike the majority of working people who must accumulate their hourly wages over a tediously long period.

The four variants of Follow system shall now be discussed in turn.

Follow Power

In a Bazi chart, the Power element is that which controls the Self. For example, Metal is the Power element of the Wood Self; Water, the Power element of Fire, and so on, as discussed in Chapter Two.

The Power element, metaphorically depicted as the ruler or tyrant of the Self, signifies pressure and leadership. When the leading flow is dictated by the Power element, such a Self then falls into a Follow Power energy system. Some Bazi schools in the West refer to the Power element as Direct Officer or Seven Killings.

Follow Power Selves are arguably the most intelligent of all Follow types, numbering many Nobel Prize-winning physicists among their ranks. The Bazi of the world's top billionaire, Bill Gates, is a classic example of this configuration. We do not include his Bazi as an illustration here, however, due to the lack of samples with a duplicate birth date.

WANG JIANLIN
B. OCTOBER 24, 1954 (SICHUAN, CHINA)

H	D	M	Y
n/a	r癸	T甲	T甲
n/a	g丑	H戌	F午

BAZI SYSTEM · FOLLOW POWER

	15	25	35	45	55
LUCK CYCLE	F丙	f丁	E戊	e己	M庚
	R子	g丑	T寅	t卯	W辰

Wang Jianlin has a Bazi very similar to that of Bill Gates, and the bonus of having four other individuals born on the same date for comparison. In 2015, he was named the richest person in China, though by 2018 he had fallen out of the top three ranking.

Born in Sichuan, China, he is currently the Chairman of the Dalian Wanda Group, China's largest real estate developer, as well as the world's largest movie theater operator. Over the years, Wang has served as a delegate and member of many government organizations, and is a leading philanthropist in China.

The Self is a feeble Yin Water, which is characterized by rain, and born in a Dog month containing the most powerful Earth in a year. With three Earth signs, and a Fire alliance empowered by the substantial flow of Wood, the Water Self in cosmic terms is absolutely helpless, thereby granting him the most desirable type of Follow configuration.

His chart contains two leading flows. The three Earth elements, tightly aligned as a team and supported by Fire, makes him a Follow

Power type. The Fire alliance of the Horse and Dog, supported by two Yang Woods, also qualifies him as a Follow Wealth type. Fortunately, these two forces are complementary and mutually supportive. This unique cosmic collaboration produces an individual of high caliber - financially astute, competent and strategic in his dealings.

His beneficial elements are essentially Fire and Earth. By nature or intuition, Wang chose real estate (Earth) and film (Fire) as his investment ventures, further empowering these beneficial flows. Clearly, the path of least cosmic resistance has made him an unmitigated success in his chosen fields.

His harmful element is Water, which antagonizes his providers by extinguishing Fire and diluting Earth. We can see why he was unable to receive a college education until his late twenties; that is, only after he stepped out of the Rat (Water) period which lasted from the ages of 20 to 24. The Water also kept him working hard in the army. How can the pair of Yang Woods in his chart be interpreted? By strict definition, it hurts his Earth. However, in this instance, as both are providentially sitting above the Fire team, they are diverted from having to control Earth to fuelling the Fire instead. The bearer of such a fortuitous configuration would be a great problem solver, adept at transforming obstacles into opportunity and advantage. Yang Wood, being also the talent or fame element of a Yin Water Self, positioned as a pair and standing tall in his Bazi, makes his prestige extend far beyond China.

YEAR	AGE	LUCK CYCLE	KEY EVENTS
Pre-1969	<25	Mostly Rat, R子	In the People's Army; studied
1986	32	Ox, g丑	Graduated (Liaoning)
1986-89	32-35	Ox, g丑	Director of a government office in Dalian City

YEAR	AGE	LUCK CYCLE	KEY EVENTS
1989	35	Yang Earth, E戊	Started real estate business
1993	39	Yang Earth, E戊	Chairman of the Board of Directors of Dalian Wanda Group Shareholding Company
2013	59	Yang Metal, M庚	Acquired British yacht maker, Sunseeker, planning to build 200 meter-high luxury hotel on London's South Bank
2014	60	Dragon, W辰	Built American headquarters of his entertainment company in Beverly Hills
2015	61	Dragon, W辰	Richest man in China

We can see from the table that Wang graduated from college as soon as he moved into the Ox (Earth) period; he prospered especially during an Earth year or Earth luck cycle, with Dragon (Yang Earth) years being the most remarkable.

Such a wonderful Bazi practically creates a blessed life or great success for all those possessing it, provided of course that they do not happen to have a watery birth hour or live by the waterfront. Four other famous individuals born on the same day offer additional perspectives on the system.

Malcolm Bligh Turnbull is the 29th Prime Minister of Australia. Turnbull's system shares the negative impact that Water had on Wang's early life: he suffered from asthma as a young child and his parents separated when he was nine in 1963 (this being a Water and

Wood year), putting him in the sole care of his father. Nevertheless, he was fortunate in being able to earn a law degree in Sydney as well as further his legal training at Oxford as a Rhodes Scholar. He also managed to practice law and sustain a career as an investment banker thereafter, while Wang kept a far lower profile serving in the Chinese army. What made the crucial difference?

No single factor is responsible for these disparities. What we do know is that a combination of the physical, socio-political and financial conditions in Sydney during the 1960s and 1970s certainly conferred greater beneficial flows upon him than did that of Wang's China.

As with Wang, he prospered with the onset of Earth, successfully establishing himself as the Chairman of the Australian Republican Movement in 1993 to 2000, a Yang Earth period. He took on the career-defining role as Australia's prime minister during the Dragon luck cycle, which was also responsible for the upswing in Wang's fortunes during this time.

Thomas Joseph "Tom" Mulcair is another practicing lawyer and lecturer of law. He has been the leader of the New Democratic Party of Canada since 2012. The negative Water impact can be seen here too, with Mulcair struggling during his law school education from the age of 18. He had to borrow money from his sister to buy textbooks, as well as pay his way through school by undertaking strenuous construction work, tarring and graveling roofs. He succeeded in becoming a party leader during his Dragon (Earth) period in 2012, which also happened to be a Dragon year.

Bradley James "Brad" Sherman is an American politician, and has been a Democratic member of the United States House of Representatives since 1997, a year of Fire and Earth, the same auspicious flow shared by his counterparts. He currently represents

California's 30th congressional district within the San Fernando Valley, in Los Angeles County, California.

Like his counterparts, he is academic and intellectual, garnering a B.A. in Political Science from University of California, Los Angeles, and a J.D. from Harvard Law School.

Douglas Donald "Doug" Davidson is an American television actor, who has portrayed private investigator Paul Williams on the CBS soap opera *The Young and the Restless* since May 1978, making him the series' longest-serving current cast member.

The year 1978 (EF戊午) had extremely powerful Earth and Fire, boosting his career prospects and placing him in a prime position to capitalize on these beneficial flows. His longevity in a typically fickle industry certainly reflects the power conferred by a Power boss in a Follow Power chart. Tellingly, Davidson also won awards in the years 1990, 1991, 1997, 2013: all the Fire/Earth years.

Follow Children

The Children element is the output or product of the Self, which behaves in figurative terms as a parent would nurture its own offspring. For example, Wood is the child of Water as Water cultivates Wood; Fire is the child of Wood as Wood generates Fire, and so on. The offspring of each elemental Self is listed in Figure 2h in Chapter Two. When the Offspring element becomes a chart's dominant flow, the Self will belong to a Follow Children configuration.

As children love and respect their parents according to natural law, Follow Children Selves are considered to have an easygoing boss, enjoying a relatively laid-back life and being granted the latitude to develop fine tastes and styles. Those operating on such a system include many queens and princesses, musicians and Nobel Prize winners in the field of medicine and economics.

KATHY IRELAND
B. MARCH 20, 1963 (CALIFORNIA, USA)

H	D	M	Y
n/a	R壬	t乙	r癸
n/a	H戌	t卯	t卯

BAZI SYSTEM · FOLLOW CHILDREN

	5	15	25	35	45	55
LUCK CYCLE	F丙	f丁	E戊	e己	M庚	m辛
	W辰	f巳	F午	d未	M申	m酉

Ireland is an American model and actress turned author and entrepreneur. She was a supermodel in the 1980s and 1990s, amassing a personal fortune of 420 million dollars by 2015 (*Forbes*). In 2012, the annual revenue of her company's retail sales stood at 2 billion dollars.

The Self is Yang Water born in spring when the flow of Wood dominates the cosmos. Her chart contains three Wood elements in a tightly bound unity that is well nurtured by rain, powerfully enfeebling the Self. In addition, the Self is being curtailed by strong Fire and Earth contained within the Dog beneath it (H戌). The feeble Self therefore adopts the Follow Children chart configuration.

Interestingly, the Follow Children system has a unique feature: the Self prospers most of all with the arrival of a grandchild - in this case, when Ireland encounters a Fire year or a Fire luck cycle. Hence, as the Water Self (parent) generates the Wood (child) which then begets Fire (grandchild) in an unbroken breeding sequence, so Ireland is cosmically poised to receive extensive and lasting blessings during these periods.

In conclusion, Ireland benefits from Wood and Fire, but dreads Water and Metal. Since Earth, with its absorptive qualities, shields her from an attack by Water, it too is beneficial. Her key life events are listed below for verification.

YEAR	AGE	LUCK CYCLE	KEY EVENTS
1974	11	Dragon, W辰	Worked on a paper route
1979	16	Yin Fire, f丁	Modeling
1980-90s	17-30s	Yin Fire, f丁	Supermodel
1993	32	Yang Earth, E戊	Founded *Kathy Ireland Worldwide*, becoming one of the wealthiest models in the world
2004	41	Goat, d未	*Kathy Ireland Worldwide* marketed products from 16 manufacturers, with annual revenue of $10 million
2012	49	Yang Metal, M庚	Ireland's company grew to approximately $2 billion in annual sales, becoming a leader in its industry

From her case history, we can see that she began modeling in a Goat year (1979) which formed a Wood alliance with the two Rabbits (t卯), succeeding quickly at age 17 during a Yin Fire period (symbolically, the grandchild of the Self as discussed). She continued to prosper for the next 25 years. Her exponential growth came during the Goat (d未) period, in alignment with the growing momentum of the Wood team.

Starting from the age of 49, however, her chart underwent a system change once under the sway of a powerful Metal and Water period (M 申). Being empowered by the Metal and able to team up with another Yang Water which joined the Yin Water (r 亥) in her chart, the once feeble Self gained strength, no longer subject to the dominant flow of another element - instead, she became Dominant Water.

Two individuals, born on the same day as Ireland, both enjoyed long-lasting acting careers.

Anouk Grinberg, a French actress, has appeared in more than 40 films and television shows since 1976; her big break came just three years prior to that of Ireland. While the latter founded her company in 1993, Grinberg won the Silver Bear Award for Best Actress at the 46th Berlin International Film Festival in 1996, another three year gap between the pair. Both have glamour and charisma in abundance, benefiting from their Fire output flow to succeed.

David Thewlis is an English actor, author, film director, and screenwriter. Like Ireland, he began work on his first film in 1987 (ft 丁 卯), a Fire and Wood (Rabbit) year, and has had a continuously productive career since.

His breakout role was also in 1993 at the age of 30 (specifically the Rat luck period). Thewlis won five awards for *Naked* (1993) that year, as well as Best Actor at the Cannes Film Festival. In 2007, a Pig year which created a Wood alliance, he published a book.

All three are widely considered beautiful, charismatic individuals, well suited to stardom, and all rightly using the Fire flow for creative expression, fame and visibility. Disparities in the momentum of financial success between Ireland and her counterparts, however, are beyond the remit of Bazi. We may conclude that while auspicious charts bestow fruitful and prosperous lives upon their bearers, momentum is down to individual initiative and entrepreneurship.

Follow Resource

The Resource element is one which supports the Self in the role of a nurturing mother. When it appears as part of an alliance or team, the individual enjoys unconditional and consistent support from a variety of sources. It translates into considerable success that comes easily via the timely assistance of many helping hands. In figurative terms, drawing from the customs of ancient China, the Self can be likened to a single male heir whose father's many wives (legal and natural mothers of the child) would have had to indulge this only child in order to gain the favor and support of their husband, and eventually the child too, once he comes to take control the family assets. The system is literally termed *Many Mothers Supporting Only Child* in Chinese.

However, this Self does not go completely unchallenged: certain "mothers" may be less devoted or benevolent than others, and the appearance of an additional male heir could have the unintended effect of toppling the support network. In such a scenario, the mothers will typically adopt a wait-and-see approach so as to re-evaluate which of the two ought to be their rightful heir, tightening the purse strings in the meantime. The two potential heirs understand their dilemma: one will have to be ousted from the family. They must therefore engage in combat until either the Self or the intruder is removed from the family.

This would explain why a Wood Self belonging to a Follow Resource configuration will typically experience changes of environment and other unfavorable conditions on encountering another Wood element. These include loss of financial support, illness and pain - a corollary of the cosmic infighting taking place between the rivals.

Persons with a Follow Resource chart configuration are likely to be observant, intuitive, congenial, attractive, and especially respectful to older women: they utilize these qualities to make each mother happy in order to gain their support.

ALISHER USMANOV
B. SEPTEMBER 9, 1953 (CHUST, UZBEKISTAN)

H	D	M	Y
n/a	r癸	m辛	r癸
n/a	r亥	m酉	f巳

BAZI SYSTEM · FOLLOW RESOURCE

	11	21	31	41	51	61
LUCK CYCLE	e己	E戊	f丁	F丙	t乙	T甲
	d未	F午	f巳	W辰	t卯	T寅

Usmanov built his wealth through Metal and mining operations, and investments, and is the majority shareholder of Metalloinvest, a Russian industrial conglomerate. He owns the Kommersant Publishing Houses and co-owns MegaFon (Russia's second-largest mobile telephone operator) and the Mail.ru group (the largest internet company in the Russian-speaking world).

The Self is Yin Water. Supported by a Metal team of m辛/m酉/ f巳, it qualifies as a Follow Resource type. Usmanov has one more Yin Water (r癸) in his year pillar, competing for the mothers' support. Some Bazi practitioners would consider this a Sibling Rivalry configuration as there are additional Water signs to compete with the Water Self, such as the aforementioned Yin Water (r癸) in the year stem - apparently not a straightforward system. How do we know where to draw the line? While there are frequently mixed systems to be found, the proper approach is to go by the useful elements. In a Sibling Rivalry chart, the Resource element is always harmful to the

Self as it promotes competition. In a Follow Resource type, however, the Resource element is always the most beneficial.

It is plain to see that Usmanov has benefited entirely through Metal, his Resource element. Metaphorically, Metal, like a doting mother, arrives in the form of a team bearing abundant resources with which to nurture and cultivate the child of the family. The child, in his turn, must please the mothers to maintain their support and protection. As such, this Bazi has produced an individual who achieves great success swiftly and naturally, becoming rich and famous over time. Metal is his vital support.

Let's verify this by referring to his case history. We can see that Usmanov was able to build his wealth through metal and mining operations, through successful investments (Metal), and as the majority shareholder of Metalloinvest (Metal business).

He had a mobile life during adolescence. Born in Uzbekistan in the provincial town of Chust, he spent his childhood in the capital, Tashkent, where his father was a state prosecutor. He later moved to Moscow to study and graduated with a degree in international law, before returning to Tashkent to embark on his career. Symbolically, he was being ousted by the Yin Water of his year pillar during this time, which led to a measure of instability and frequent movement.

The worst event, however, took place in 1980 when he was imprisoned for six years under mysterious circumstances. By 2000, he had been exonerated, the original charge being deemed a wrongful accusation based on fabricated data. What does this signify in cosmic terms? Usmanov was 27 in 1980, during the luck cycle of the Horse (Fire). The strong Fire which began at the age of 26, and which continued for five years, extended into the next Yin Fire period, burning and threatening all the mothers in the process, who in their turn, clubbed together to have him imprisoned as a punishment.

He was released in 1985 (tg乙丑), an Ox year, when the Ox (a Metal house) joined the partial alliance of Snake and Rooster in his Bazi to make a full Metal team. Symbolically, a new and more influential mother arrived on the scene to pull the angry mothers together and forgive their wayward son. Remarkably, in 2000 (MW庚辰), once again a year of potent Metal, an all-powerful new mother, in the form of Yang Metal, came along to clear the wrongful record.

Let us check on the key events of his career to find out more. After the wrongful imprisonment and from the age of 37, he quickly established himself as the director and chairman of several notable firms (1990 to 1998). Why? The Snake period from ages 36 to 40 reinforced his Metal team and concurrently pushed away another hidden Yang Water in the Pig, his competitor, enhancing his winning ability to gain support. Fortunately, the Yang Fire in the following period which governed ages 41 to 45 was absorbed by one of the caring mothers, that is, the Yin Metal in the stem. From the age of 46, the onset of powerful Earth from the Dragon followed by 15 years of Wood flow all combined to drain Water for his protection, paving his way to lasting prosperity.

YEAR	AGE	LUCK CYCLE	KEY EVENTS
1976	23	Yang Earth, E戊	Graduated in international law. appointed Director of the Foreign Economic Association of the Soviet Peace Committee
1980	27	Horse, F午	Imprisoned for six years
1990-94	37-41	Snake, f巳	Deputy General Director of Intercross JSC
1994-1998	41-45	Yang Fire, F丙	Headed Interfin Interbank; Advisor to the General Director of Moscow Aviation Industrial Enterprise

YEAR	AGE	LUCK CYCLE	KEY EVENTS
2015	62	Rabbit, t卯	Russia's richest man, with a fortune estimated at $14.7 billion, and the world's 58th richest person (*Forbes*)

Born on the same day is **Janet Fielding**, an Australian actress who has had a successful and versatile career. Strikingly, her life events also demonstrate the clear impact of Metal, Fire and Water. Here is her luck cycle in the female order for illustration.

	10	20	30	40	50
LUCK CYCLE	R壬	r癸	T甲	t乙	F丙
	H戌	r亥	R子	g丑	T寅

She began acting in 1980 (MM庚申), and was cast as the next *Doctor Who* companion in 1981 (mm辛酉), both years characterized by powerful Metal flow. In 1991, aged 38, she went through a divorce and change of career. This took place during a stressful Water period in the wake of the burning effects of the Horse from the foregoing year (1990, MF庚午). Fortunately, with the onset of a Metal trio formation during the Ox period, when Fielding was in her late forties, she embarked on a new career in PR, participating in a series of visible projects.

At 50, the Yang Fire period set in, and in 2006 (FH丙戌), aged 53, she lost her PR industry connections which placed her under pressure to return to acting. By 2012, a watery year taking place at the tail end of her Fire period, sources revealed that the actress had been battling cancer.

Follow Wealth

The Wealth element is that which the Self controls, as Fire is to a Water Self, for example. A Follow Wealth Self follows the dominant element of Wealth for protection and provision. Thus, a feeble Wood Self would follow the lead of Earth; a Metal Self would follow Wood, Water would follow Fire, and so on.

ANGELA MERKEL
B. JULY 17, 1954 (HAMBURG, GERMANY)

Merkel, has been the Chancellor of Germany since 2005, the first woman to hold this office.

H	D	M	Y
n/a	T甲	m辛	T甲
n/a	H戌	d未	F午

BAZI SYSTEM • FOLLOW WEALTH/FOLLOW CHILDREN

	13	23	33	43	53	63
LUCK CYCLE	e己	E戊	f丁	F丙	t乙	T甲
	f巳	W辰	t卯	T寅	g丑	R子

As a Yang Wood born in July at the height of summer, the Self is weak. Earth, in three consecutive branches, becomes its leading flow, rendering the Self a Follow Wealth type. On the other hand, with the Fire alliance of the Dog and the Horse, a Fire trio could be formed with the missing Tiger quite easily, rendering her a Follow Children as well. She became Germany's Chancellor in 2005, the peak of her

Fire Trio, the Tiger period. Regardless, Earth is the fundamental leading flow.

Thus, Earth and Fire are her most auspicious elements. Wood which challenges her Earth is harmful. In 2011 at the age of 57 (a Rabbit year occurring during her Yin Wood period), a poll found her coalition had only 36 per cent approval. The minute she entered the Ox (Earth) period at the age of 58, however, she was rated the world's second most powerful person by *Forbes*. In 2015, during the same Ox period, she was named *TIME* magazine's Person of the Year, which emphatically declared her "Chancellor of the Free World."

YEAR	AGE	LUCK CYCLE	KEY EVENTS
1978-1990	24-36	Yang Earth-Yin Fire, EW-f 戊辰-丁	Received a doctorate degree; worked at Central Institute for Physical Chemistry of the Academy of Sciences in Berlin-Adlershof
1991	37	Yin Fire, f 丁	Minister for Women and Youth under Chancellor Helmut Kohl
2005	51	Tiger, 丁寅	Germany's first female chancellor
2011	57	Rabbit, t 卯	Poll found her coalition only had 36% approval
2012	58	Ox, g 丑	World's second most powerful person (*Forbes*)
2015	61	Ox, g 丑	*TIME* magazine's Person of the Year, "Chancellor of the Free World"

Her duplicate birth counterparts are both male:

Richard Dale Barnes is a distinguished head basketball coach. He has had a successful and uninterrupted career as a coach in basketball since 1977 and as head coach since 1987 in teams all over the United States. Sport is Fire by the five elements classification.

J. Michael Straczynski is an American writer and producer. He works in films, television series, novels, short stories, comic books, radio dramas and other media, which in the main are all Fire-related careers.

VARIABLE

The nature and function of a Variable system has been discussed in the opening section of this chapter. We will move to the illustration of an example:

SAULI NIINISTÖ
B. AUGUST 24, 1948 (SALO, FINLAND)

Niinistö was a practicing lawyer prior to becoming the twelfth president of Finland. Besides having an auspicious Variable system, his chart also has three further beneficial features, placing him ahead of the herd. Firstly, as a Yin Metal Self born in a Monkey month, he is blessed with attraction and intelligence. Secondly, with a day pillar of mf辛巳 falling into the Strategically Intelligent,[2] he is very resourceful. Thirdly, his year pillar, ER戊子, puts him in a high position: a Bazi code says that a Yin Metal Self with a Yang Earth Rat pillar in the birth chart (at any position) will succeed easily in achieving fame or high status.

H	D	M	Y
n/a	m辛	M庚	E戊
n/a	f巳	M申	R子

BAZI SYSTEM · VARIABLE

	15	25	35	45	55	65
LUCK CYCLE	R壬	r癸	T甲	t乙	F丙	f丁
	H戌	r亥	R子	g丑	T寅	t卯

2 See Chapter Three, p.33.

It is a Variable system for the following reasons:

1. As a Metal Self surrounded by three more Metal elements, this is a classic Sibling Rivalry case.
2. He could be a Dominant Metal upon the onset of either a g丑 or m酉 in the branches.
3. He has the opportunity to become a Follow Children type when the stem of M庚, his biggest drawback in the chart, is removed. This is the most promising system for him to prosper.

Before the age of 29, as a competitive Metal under the sway of a Sibling Rivalry configuration, he had to work hard to elbow competing Metals out of the way (that is, competitors in reality) to become a lawyer.

At 29 in 1977 (ff丁巳), a strong Fire year which melted down the Yang Metal stem, he became a Follow Children type, finally taking his first steps into politics by serving the Municipal council.

A similar formation took place in 1995 (tr乙亥), when Niinistö was 47 during his Yin Wood period. The powerful Yin Wood succeeded in eliminating Yang Metal completely by pairing up with it. With the sudden change to a Follow Children configuration, Niinistö rose to become head of the Justice Department of Finland and soon after, the Minister of Finance. From ages 49 to 54, the Ox from his luck cycle joined the Snake to form a Metal team, making him Dominant Metal again. It solidified his position, readying his leadership for the next move.

The Dragon year of 2012 saw the Dragon joining forces with his Rat and Monkey. With the full Water trio, Niinistö became a fully-qualified Follow Children type once more - in fact, he became President of Finland.

YEAR	AGE	LUCK CYCLE	KEY EVENTS
1977	29	Pig, r亥	Served in the Municipal Council
1987	39	Rat, R子	Member of the Parliament of Finland in his district until 1992
1995	47	Yin Wood, t乙	Justice Minister in Prime Minister Paavo Lipponen's first cabinet
1996-2002	48-54	Ox, g丑	Minister of Finance
2002-2011	54-63	Yang Fire, F丙	Honorary President of the European People's Party
2012	64	Rabbit, t卯	President of Finland

Four people were born on the same day as Niinistö. Interestingly, three are also Europeans, all talented.

Vicente "Tito" Castelo Sotto III shared Niinistö's aptitude for politics. An actor, comedian, singer, songwriter, TV host, and journalist, he was also Vice Mayor of Quezon City in the Philippines from 1988 to 1992 (during the Ox period), and three terms senate from 1992 to 2004 (the Fire periods), ably demonstrating the versatility of individuals with Variable energy systems.

Alexander McCall Smith, born in Southern Rhodesia (present-day Zimbabwe), shared Niinistö's legal aptitude and skills of execution. He earned a Ph.D in law and became Emeritus Professor of Medical Law at the University of Edinburgh, serving on various British and international committees in this field.

In later years, he became a well-known writer, publishing thirty books during the 1980s and 1990s (his Ox period included). He was awarded an honorary degree of Doctor of Laws from the University of Edinburgh School of Law in 2007, and another of Doctor of Letters in 2015.

Jean Michel Jarre from Lyon enjoyed the Metal–Water effects. He is a French composer, performer, and music producer, first encountering mainstream success in 1976 with *Oxygène*, which sold over 12 million copies. The Dragon of 1976 joined his Rat and Monkey to form a full Water trio. As of 2004, a year when the Monkey came to reinforce his Water team, Jarre has sold an estimated 80 million albums.

Nana Jorjadze, the only female in the group, is a Georgian film director, scriptwriter and actress. Her debut as an actress came in 1977, the same year that the Finnish President embarked on politics. She won the Caméra d'Or at the 1987 Cannes Film Festival, just as Niinistö gained a foothold in the Finnish Parliament. She directed many films, one of which became the first, and so far the only, Georgian film to be nominated for the Academy Award in 1996, a year when the Rat made her Dominant Water.

§

We now have an understanding of the common Bazi systems shared by so many of today's notable personalities. Several have succeeded with additional features besides simply a good Bazi. The special stars discussed in Chapter Three, for example, play a remarkable role in pushing people to succeed; thus when analyzing a Bazi, one also needs to pinpoint these special features as a crucial reference point.

For discussions on the examples in the next four chapters, we will use the same format, starting with the Bazi pillars and luck cycles, its analysis supported by key life events, and comparisons of those with duplicate birth dates.

CHAPTER FIVE

DUPLICATE BIRTHS WITH COMPARABLE PATHS

We have selected 17 examples of notable figures for discussion, drawn from an international pool of talent. Together with their birth counterparts, these have been divided into two groups, and their case histories presented across the current chapter and the next. Our intention is not to overwhelm readers with too much material at once, but rather that each chapter provides the breathing space needed to fully digest its themes. This dividing line is not arbitrary: the first nine case studies have comparable histories, whilst the second group of eight have contrasting ones. Although every example shares common traits with their birth duplicates, many have variations of momentum in their achievements and career arcs, which have enabled us to loosely group our examples into two.

§

1 SIR JERRY MATEPARAE
B. NOVEMBER 14, 1954 (WHANGANUI, NEW ZEALAND)

Jerry Mateparae is New Zealand's 20th Governor-General, the second Māori person to hold this office. As a fellow of the New Zealand Institute of Management, he also has a master's degree in International Relations and Strategic Studies from the University of Waikato.

Born in the Whanganui, Mateparae was raised in a major urban hilly settlement on the lower banks of the Whanganui River, the longest navigable waterway in the country. The region is known for its outstanding natural environment - temperate, with enough humidity to promote vegetation, it is rich in Wood flow.

H	D	M	Y
n/a	T甲	t乙	T甲
n/a	H戌	r亥	F午

BAZI SYSTEM · SIBLING RIVALRY

	17	27	37	47	57	67
LUCK CYCLE	f丁	E戊	e己	M庚	m辛	R壬
	g丑	T寅	t卯	W辰	f巳	F午

The Self is Yang Wood. Born in a Wood month and surrounded by three individual Woods, yet no Wood team, it is a Sibling Rivalry case denoting a combative, unstable life. There are two ways to succeed in this scenario. Firstly, Metal or Fire may be used to curtail the Wood Siblings - his competitors. Secondly, a Rabbit or a Goat may join his Pig, and in so doing, render him a Wood team leader. Earth, representing the money which tempts the Wood elements to combat, is very detrimental.

Before the age of 40, during his mainly Earth periods, Mateparae worked and studied, struggling to gain a foothold in the national armed forces. Even then, he seemed to make minimal headway in terms of army career progression, advancing from Lieutenant to Major.

With the approach of his Rabbit period after the age of 40, Mateparae became Dominant Wood. His luck turned and he was promoted to Commander. The positive effects of the Rabbit period were happily succeeded by the Yang Metal, which powerfully curtailed his Wood Siblings. With the Siblings under control or defeated, Mateparae marched on to become Chief of Army. Finally, during his own Metal period in 2011, a year of Metal Rabbit, he was able to round up all the Wood and join them in a team under his sole command, becoming Dominant Wood once more. This double dose of fortune paved the way for Mateparae to become leader of the country.

Throughout his career, and of the 12 major awards he received, a third fell into the two Rabbit years of his lifetime. Being raised in a Wood-rich environment, his own stock of Wood flow was rich enough to reinforce the onset of additional Wood flows, capitalizing on them to wondrous effect.

YEAR	AGE	LUCK CYCLE	KEY EVENTS
1976-1994	22-40	Earth, g丑-ET戊 寅-e己	Lowest-ranking officer in the national army
1994-1998	40-44	Transition to Rabbit, t卯	Commanded Peace Monitoring Group on Bougainville during Operation Belisi

YEAR	AGE	LUCK CYCLE	KEY EVENTS
1999-2001	45-47	Rabbit-Yang Metal, t卯-M庚	Joint Commander of New Zealand forces attached to the UN Transitional Administration in East Timor
2002-2006	48-52	Yang Metal, M庚	Chief of General Staff (title later changed to Chief of Army)
2006-2011	52-57	Dragon, W辰	Chief of the New Zealand Defense Force
2011	57	Yin Metal, m辛	Appointed Governor-General

Condoleezza Rice, State Secretary of the United States, was born in Birmingham, Alabama, USA, on the same day as Mateparae. As with Mateparae, she rose from a minority background to become a prominent politician of her country. Remarkably, she was also born and raised in a hilly city with a subtropical climate and abundant rainfall. However, Rice's rise to prominence was aided by the sunnier environment of her birthplace.

To see how the flow worked in her life, we need to display her luck cycle and key life events for easy comparison.

	12	22	32	42	52
LUCK CYCLE	r癸	R壬	m辛	M庚	e己
	m酉	M申	d未	F午	f巳

YEAR	AGE	LUCK CYCLE	KEY EVENTS
1980	26	Monkey, M申	Ph.D in political science, University of Denver
1980-1981	26-27	Monkey, M申	Soviet studies at Stanford University, on a Ford Foundation Fellowship
1981-1993	27-39	Monkey-Yin Metal-Dominant Wood, M 申-m辛-d未	Assistant/associate professor of political science at Stanford University
2001-2005	47-51	Horse, F午	National Security Adviser in the White House
2005-2008	51-54	Horse, F午	Secretary of State
2009	55	Yin Earth, e己	Returned to Stanford University

In 1981, a powerful Metal year taking place during her Metal luck cycle, she began teaching at Stanford University, holding the position for the 12 years that spanned her Metal and Dominant Wood periods.

Rice is also fortunate in having the crucially beneficial elements crowded into the prime window of her life, bringing a slew of successes early on in her career. The compounding effects of the Goat period from ages 37 to 41, the Yang Metal at age 46, and the Fire at age 51, all helped to bring about and cement this success, granting her a visibility that attracted the attention of the White House. (Mateparae, on the other hand, had to wait until the age of 57 to experience it.) In another marked similarity, both also studied International Business.

With two Red-light pillars (TH甲戌 and TF甲午) between them, both have had to deal with a degree of challenge to their relationships. While Mateparae married twice, Rice remains unattached.

2 VLADIMIR PUTIN
B. OCTOBER 7, 1952 (LENINGRAD, SOVIET UNION)

Vladimir Putin was born in Leningrad (now St. Petersburg). He has served as both Prime Minister and President of the Russian Federation at various times since 1999, and as of 2018 remains in office. After graduating from Leningrad State University in 1975, he began his career in the KGB as an intelligence officer, stationed mainly in East Germany, until 1989.

H	D	M	Y
n/a	F丙	e己	R壬
n/a	H戌	m酉	W辰

BAZI SYSTEM · FOLLOW CHILDREN

	11	21	31	41	51	61
LUCK CYCLE	m辛	R壬	r癸	T甲	t乙	F丙
	r亥	R子	g丑	T寅	t卯	W辰

The Self is a Yang Fire, born in the fall which is afflicted by declining sunlight. With three Earths draining its feeble strength and Water weakening it further, he surrenders to the Earth, becoming a Follow Children. The chart enjoys more Earth, while Water, reflecting the glamour of the sun and having the added effect of enfeebling the Self, is also welcome. Metal presents financial gain. He dreads Fire, especially Yang Fire which disrupts his Follow status. However, given the freezing cold environment of Russia, the Fire impact will be minimal. Wood could present challenges as it empowers the Self to rebel and hurts his beneficial Earth. Fortunately, Wood is considered a rare species in Russia since the cold environment is not supportive of its growth.

Putin possesses a fabulous system. Indeed, a number of its unique features have barely been discussed in English Bazi literature. To begin with, he owns two of the most fortunate pillars among the sixty-pillar group. The Dragon of his year pillar (RW壬辰) is embraced by the Yang Water's two Noblemen (the Rabbit and Snake), while the day pillar, Yang Fire Dog (FH丙戌), has its Dog embraced by the Yang Fire's two Noblemen (the Rooster and Pig). This configuration brings great fortune.

The month pillar (em己酉) is one of the four Promotional Pillars in the sixty-pillar group.[1] A Promotional Pillar encourages ambition and swift easy success. It is best found in the month and day pillar as its impact extends over the entire lifetime. Being a Follow Type as well as having such fortunate pillars in his possession, Putin's measure of good fortune is providentially twofold.

The Dragon in his Bazi could also lead to great fortune. As a Yang Fire Self, Putin has the "Tiger and the Dragon" as his pairing stars for Fame and Wealth.[2] All that is required is the onset of a Tiger to succeed. During his Tiger period from the ages of 46 to 50, he experienced the greatest career progression of his life, moving from Deputy Chief of Presidential Staff under President Boris Yeltsin, all the way to becoming President in just five years.

From his life events, we can see that even during his worst period (the Yang Wood from ages 41 to 45), he was unemployed for perhaps only one to two years, before finding a job in the local government. Not long after he stepped out from Yang Wood, he became a department head of the nation.

The period of Yang Fire from ages 61 to 65 was challenging, seeing Putin under siege on all fronts with both domestic and interna-

---

1 Refer to Chapter Three, p.34, for further information.
2 See Chapter Three, p.32 for Wealth pairing stars.

tional issues. Nevertheless, his position as both a national and world leader remains undisputed.

YEAR	AGE	LUCK CYCLE	KEY EVENTS
1975-1989	23-37	Rat-Yin Water, R子-r癸	Intelligence officer in the KGB, East Germany
1994-1996	42-44	Yang Wood, T甲	Sobchak's first deputy mayor
1998	46	Tiger, T寅	Deputy head of management under Yeltsin's administration
1999	47	Tiger, T寅	Prime Minister
2000	48	Tiger, T寅	President
2004	52	Yin Wood, t乙	President
2008	56	Rabbit, t卯	Prime Minister
2012	60	Rabbit, t卯	President

Ludmilla Ivanovna Tourischeva is a former Russian gymnast and nine-time Olympic medalist for the Soviet Union.

From 1970 to 1974, Tourischeva dominated almost every major international competition, winning the World Championships all-around gold in 1970 and 1974, the European Championships in 1971 and 1973, and the World Cup in 1975. She was considered the embodiment of classic Soviet style: grace, elegance, impeccable form and strong technique.

Tourischeva has received many accolades for her contributions to gymnastics, including the Women In Sport trophy by the International Olympic Committee. As Putin is a world leader in the field of politics, so Tourischeva is a queen in the world of sports. This is the beauty of a great Bazi.

Despite the diverging luck cycle energy, they did share one banner year. In 1998, she was inducted into the International Gymnastics Hall of Fame, the same year that Putin made his vital step into the First Circle of national politics, becoming the Deputy Chief of Presidential Staff under Yeltsin. The Tiger of that year assisted them both at the same time.

3 MARGARET "MEG" WHITMAN
B. AUGUST 4, 1956 (NEW YORK, USA)

Margaret Whitman, a native of Huntington, New York, is an American business executive, political activist and philanthropist, perhaps best known for having been the CEO of eBay. She was also the chairwoman, president, and CEO of Hewlett-Packard from September 2011 to February 2018.

The Self is Yin Water. Drained by a Wood team comprised of Yin Wood, the Rabbit and the Goat (t乙/t卯/d未) which forms the dominant flow of her system, she possesses mostly a Follow Children Bazi configuration. However, the Sibling Yang Water, hidden in the Monkey of her year pillar could potentially render the system that of Sibling Rivalry in early life. On the other hand, the powerful Monkey also has the potential to form a Water team upon the onset of a Dragon or a Rat. This process would then transform the Self into Dominant Water.

H	D	M	Y
n/a	r癸	t乙	F丙
n/a	t卯	d未	M申

BAZI SYSTEM · VARIABLE

	19	29	39	49	59	69
LUCK CYCLE	r癸	R壬	m辛	M庚	e己	E戊
	f巳	W辰	t卯	T寅	g丑	R子

Her beneficial elements are Wood and, occasionally, Water, depending on the circumstances. Let us take a look at the key events of her life.

YEAR	AGE	LUCK CYCLE	KEY EVENTS
1977	21	Yin Water, r癸	B.A., Princeton University
1979	23	Yin Water, r癸	M.B.A., Harvard Business School
1979-1989	23-33	Snake, f巳	Manager and consultant, Bain & Company
1989-1992	33-36	Dragon, W辰	Senior vice president of marketing, Stride Rite Corporation
1992-1995	36-39	Dragon, W辰	Division president, Florists' Transworld Delivery
1995-1997	39-41	Yin Metal, m辛	President and CEO, Hasbro
1998-2008	42-52	Rabbit-Yang Metal, t卯-M庚	CEO of eBay, overseeing its expansion from 30 to over 15,000 employees, and from $4 million to $8 billion in annual revenue
2011	55	Tiger, T寅	Joined Hewlett-Packard's board of directors, named CEO
2014	58	Yin Earth, e己	Listed 20th of 100 most powerful women in the world (*Forbes*)

During her Yin Water period (r癸), she fell into a Sibling Rivalry pattern, investing financial resources and time into her studies, and encountering competition in the classroom. From ages 33 to 39, with the onset of the Dragon joining her Monkey and transforming her into Dominant Water, she quickly rose to a position of prominent leadership, becoming the division president of the company.

A miracle then took place in 1998, the minute Whitman entered her Rabbit period. The Rabbit, like a troop of additional Wood sent in to empower and expand the existing Wood team, made her a great general, winning phenomenal battles during the ten years at eBay.

After 2008, she entered the Tiger period which clashed with her Monkey. A few bumpy years ensued before she was hired as the CEO of Hewlett-Packard. The year was 2011: the fortuitous Rabbit put in another appearance, landing her the position.

Iqbal Ahmed is a Bangladesh-born British entrepreneur. He moved to England at the age of 15. Joining his family business after college, he eventually founded a seafood company and made his fortune in importing shrimp, as well as from shipping, hotels, and real estate development.

Based in Manchester, he has worked his way up to become a leader in his field, playing an active role over the years in a number of government advisory bodies. He also became one of the United Kingdom's richest men and the highest ranked British Bangladeshi to be featured on the Sunday Times Rich List.

To see how the flow is working for Ahmed, here is his luck cycle and key events.

	11	21	31	41	51
LUCK CYCLE	f丁	E戊	e己	M庚	m辛
	m酉	H戌	r亥	R子	g丑

YEAR	AGE	LUCK CYCLE	KEY EVENTS
1992	36	Pig, r亥 (Wood trio)	Founder and CEO of the Seamark Group; owned hotels and restaurants
2001	45	Yang Metal, M庚	New office created in the US to distribute products in North America
2006	50	Rat, R子	In the *Sunday Times* Rich List with a net worth of GBP 110 million, and a workforce of 2000 in Bangladesh
2007	51	Rat, R子	Represented his trade members in a number of government committees and advisory bodies

The Wood team and Water team also created a similar break-through good fortune in Ahmed's life. Having been born and raised in a place close to water, and later moving to misty London, Ahmed has managed to incorporate a vast flow of Water into his system, which tends to respond more favorably to the impact of Water - he prospers naturally on sea-related products.

John Burkhalter is businessman, politician, and real estate developer from Arkansas, USA. As of 2018, he serves as president of Burkhalter Technologies, a construction business.

Both Burkhalter and Ahmed entered politics in 2007, with Burkhalter serving as Chairman of the Arkansas Economic Development Commission from 2007 to 2011.

The foregoing individuals all hold top tier positions, navigating their respective fields with a fluidity and visibility that bears out the versatile executive skills indicated by their charts.

Another fascinating example of this chart belongs to French chef, **Alain Passard,** owner of the three-star restaurant *L'Arpège* in Paris. The rich flow of Wood and Water is used to great artistic effect by Passard who plans his menus based on the seasons, sourcing natural and organic products from farmers. To further elevate the quality of his products, he created three kitchen gardens across three different *terroirs* of Western France in 2002, 2005 and 2008, suffusing the vegetables with the soil of his chosen regions. Passard's ingenuity offers us a beautiful and unique way of observing how the cosmic flow effects of this Bazi operate in real terms.

4 LEONARD LAUDER
B. MARCH 19, 1933 (NEW YORK, USA)

Leonard A. Lauder is an American businessman, the chairman emeritus of The Estée Lauder Companies Inc., and was its CEO until 1999. He is a graduate of the Wharton School of the University of Pennsylvania, and Columbia University's Graduate School of Business, and formally joined Estée Lauder in 1958 at the age of 25.

H	D	M	Y
n/a	T甲	t乙	r癸
n/a	M申	t卯	m酉

BAZI SYSTEM · SIBLING RIVALRY

LUCK CYCLE	14	24	34	44	54	64
	r癸	R壬	m辛	M庚	e己	E戊
	g丑	R子	r亥	H戌	m酉	M申

The Self as Yang Wood, surrounded by two more Wood elements, falls into a Sibling Rivalry configuration. Fortunately, as the Self is the Yang Wood supported by Water, he becomes the winning Sibling among the gang, destined to win in all fights. For big wins, however, he needs the onset of a Pig or Goat to form a Wood alliance under his leadership. Another viable, though lesser, option is to use substantial Metal to control the other Wood elements - that is, a Dog, an Ox or a Snake, to form a Metal team.

Powerful Metal did come along in 1958, a Dog year, when the Dog joined his Rooster and Monkey to form a directional Metal team which controlled the Wood. At 25, after a halting start to his career, he was finally able to focus his energy, making the bold decision to join Estée Lauder - a fortunate move indeed.

At 39, he entered his Pig (r亥) period: the Pig joined the Rabbit in the month pillar, to form a Wood team, elevating him to Dominant Wood status. He became the president of the company after 14 years of hard work. With a renewed focused energy for sound decision-making, he quickly steered the company towards its successful expansion.

At 49, Lauder entered his own Dog period, becoming Estée Lauder's CEO. Under the growing momentum of Metal for a lengthy five-year period, he continued to excel within the company. In 1995, a Pig year, another victory was scored: this time he became the company's chairman. Lined up in an unbroken succession, the good luck elements faithfully fulfilled their duty - a streak of favorable cycles was able to amend the shortfalls within his Bazi chart.

YEAR	AGE	LUCK CYCLE	KEY EVENTS
1958	25	Yang Water, R壬	Joined Estée Lauder
1972-1995	39-62	Pig, r亥	President of Estée Lauder
1982-1999	49-66	Dog, H戌	CEO of Estée Lauder
1995-2009	62-76	Yin Metal, m辛	Chairman of Estée Lauder

Four other notable individuals were born on this day, two male and two female.

Philip Roth, a famed American novelist, came closest to Lauder's life path, the two being great leaders of their fields during the 20th century. Roth hails from New Jersey, while Lauder was born in New York, both from Jewish families. They earned master's degrees from an elite university and spent some time in the United States Army before focusing on their careers.

While Lauder's good fortune began at Estée Lauder in 1958, a Dog year, Roth caught another vibrant flow just a year behind. The Pig year of 1959 established Roth as a rising star of American fiction with the publication of *Goodbye, Columbus* (1959). This work won the National Book Award and was later made into a feature film.

Now let us put Roth's award-winning years into perspective for comparison.

YEAR	AGE	LUCK CYCLE	KEY EVENTS
1969	36	Yin Metal, m辛	First best-seller, *Portnoy's Complaint* (Yin Earth Rooster year)
1995	62	Rooster, m酉	National Book Award for *Sabbath's Theater* (Yin Wood Pig year)
1997	64	Rooster, m酉	Pulitzer Prize for *American Pastoral* (Yin Fire Ox year)
2001	68	Monkey, M申	The inaugural Franz Kafka Prize (Yin Metal Snake year)

Although Roth did well during those years when a Wood team was formed, he prospered more during Metal years, as the many Metal signs indicate in the table above. Interestingly, the art of writing in ancient China evolved from the use of a metal tool with which to craft characters on wood prior to the invention of paper. Indeed, a great writer would have been nicknamed "Iron Pen" in China, a fact fairly befitting Roth's talents within his chosen field.

Lauder's cosmetics career springs from Wood and Metal. While its materials are plants and chemicals, suitably translating into Wood and Metal, the skin which absorbs the materials is also considered

Metal, somewhat dissipating its energy. Lauder's system thereby responds more favorably to Wood.

Richard Williams, a Canadian–British animator, emigrated from Toronto to London in 1955. Unfortunately, there is little in the way of detailed work by year with which to discuss his flows. Crucially, however, the effects of the powerful Dog year of 1958 also applied to Williams. In this year, he produced *The Little Island* (1958) and won the 1958 BAFTA Award for Animated Film.

Interestingly, the actress **Renee Taylor,** is also Jewish and hails from New York. She started acting in 1958, sharing a banner year with Lauder and his counterparts.

Phyllis Newman, another American actress from Jersey City, New Jersey, has similarly enjoyed a long and fruitful career.

5 DAVID BOHM
B. DECEMBER 20, 1917 (PENNSYLVANIA, USA)

David Bohm was an American scientist, whose contributions of innovative and unorthodox ideas to the fields of neuropsychology, quantum theory, and the philosophy of mind, have made him one of the most significant theoretical physicists of the 20th century.

He was born in Pennsylvania, United States, to a Hungarian-Jewish immigrant. Due to certain youthful Communist affiliations, Bohm was targeted during the McCarthy era, prompting him to leave the United States. He pursued his scientific career in several countries, becoming first a Brazilian and then a British citizen.

H	D	M	Y
n/a	F丙	R壬	f丁
n/a	M甲	R子	f巳

BAZI SYSTEM · FOLLOW POWER

	24	34	44	54	64	74
LUCK CYCLE	e己	E戊	f丁	F丙	t乙	T甲
	m酉	M申	d未	F午	f巳	W辰

The Self is Yang Fire, born in a very wet month on a wet day, sitting on a pool of Water. With the three Water signs closely knit into a strong Water team, the Fire Self follows the flow of Power, creating an individual who is at once extremely intelligent, intuitive, pleasing and attractive.

With Water as a provider and protector, Water and Metal become his beneficial elements. On the other hand, his harmful elements are

Fire (which competes with the Self for provisions), Wood (which empowers the Self thereby disrupting his Follow configuration), and Earth (which impedes the function of the Water) - all likely to create misfortune.

Bohm's happiest time was from the ages of 28 to 32, a Rooster period (Metal flow) during which he taught at Princeton, working with Einstein. As he entered the Yang Earth period, his luck changed significantly: forced to leave Princeton, Bohm took up a teaching post in Brazil. When he entered the Monkey period, with its onset of additional Metal and Water, his luck turned again. He married and relocated to England to become a research fellow at the University of Bristol. He eventually taught at Birkbeck College, University of London.

YEAR	AGE	LUCK CYCLE	KEY EVENTS
1943	26	Yin Earth, e己	Ph.D, Berkeley
1945-1949	28-32	Rooster, m酉	Assistant professor at Princeton University
1951-1954	34-37	Yang Earth, E戊	Quit Princeton, taking up a teaching post in Brazil
1955-1957	38-40	Monkey, M申	Relocated to Israel, working at Haifa, married in 1957
1957-1961	40-44	Monkey, M申	Relocated to England; research fellow at the University of Bristol
1961-1987	44-70	Yin Wood-Snake, t乙-f巳	Professor of theoretical physics at Birkbeck College, University of London

YEAR	AGE	LUCK CYCLE	KEY EVENTS
1987	70	Snake, f乙	Retired but continued to work in research

Audrey Totter, born and raised in Illinois, was an American actress. She began her acting career in radio in the late 1930s, while Bohm was busy studying at various universities. However, the two share some key turning points in their lives.

The period of 1945 to 1950 appeared to be the most successful or happiest time for them. Bohm was teaching in Princeton University from 1945 to 1949, while Totter's most successful films were made between 1946 and 1950, the height of production falling between 1947 and 1949, during which she produced three films a year.

Just as Bohm failed to keep his position at Princeton, setting off for Brazil in 1951, so the quality of Totter's films also fell in the same year. Similarly, while the itinerant Bohm was trying to improve his career prospects from 1954 to 1961, Totter struggled throughout the 1950s to make the best of a declining career. They both married late in the 1950s (unusual for a movie star, in Totter's case), and although Totter lived 21 years longer, both died of stroke.

6 LAURENE POWELL JOBS
B. NOVEMBER 6, 1963 (NEW JERSEY, USA)

H	D	M	Y
n/a	r癸	R壬	r癸
n/a	g丑	H戌	t卯

BAZI SYSTEM · VARIABLE

	11	21	31	41	51
LUCK CYCLE	T甲	t乙	F丙	f丁	E戊
	R子	g丑	T寅	t卯	W辰

Laurene Powell Jobs is an American heiress, business executive, and the founder of Emerson Collective, which advocates for policies concerning education and immigration reform, social justice, and environmental conservation. She is the widow of Steve Jobs, managing the Laurene Powell Jobs Trust. As of 2015, Powell is ranked the 45th richest person in the world by *Forbes*.

Powell Jobs earned a B.A. from the University of Pennsylvania, B.S. in Economics from the Wharton School, and M.B.A. from the Stanford Graduate School of Business. She co-founded Terravera, a natural foods company that sold to retailers throughout Northern California. Powell Jobs also worked for Merrill Lynch Asset Management and Goldman Sachs as a fixed-income trading strategist.

The Self is Yin Water. With two more Water elements on the stems, it is officially a Sibling Rivalry system. However, the Earth, being in its prime growth cycle, is too powerful for the Waters to combat as Siblings. In fact, Earth is the leading flow of the system. Earth also represents her spouse element. However, it is not strong enough to lead the Self to prosperity or success. She needs additional Earth or Fire to create a Follow Power system. Typically, a Follow Power woman is prone to marry a distinguished and successful husband.

As it turned out, she made a fortunate move by studying at Stanford University, where she met Steve Jobs, and married him in her Ox period (Earth). Following the Ox period were fifteen years of great Fire to curtail the Water and empower the Earth, during which she was able to enjoy 15 years of stable married life. However, she entered the Rabbit period (Wood) from the age of 46. As the Wood flow hurts her spouse element (Earth), her husband's health began to deteriorate. He died in a Metal Rabbit year.[3]

YEAR	AGE	LUCK CYCLE	KEY EVENTS
1985	22	Yin Wood, t乙	B.S. in economics from the Wharton School
1985-1988	22-25	Yin Wood, t乙	Worked for Merrill Lynch and Goldman Sachs
1989	26	Ox, g丑	M.B.A. from Stanford Graduate School of Business
1991-2011	28-48	Ox-Yang Fire, g 丑-F丙	Married Steve Jobs, giving birth to three children
2011	48	Rabbit, t卯	Death of husband, Steve Jobs
2014	51	Yang Earth, E 戊	Founder of various philanthropic organizations

Joy Bauer, born on the same day, stands as a very interesting case. As a consultant of nutrition and fitness, she shared Powell Jobs' in-

---

3 The Bazi of Steve Jobs was discussed in *Four Pillars of Destiny, Discover Your Code to Success* (2013)

terest in natural foods during the early part of her life. Bauer holds a bachelor's degree in Kinesiological Sciences from the University of Maryland, and a master of science in nutrition from New York University. Both are married with children.

In terms of publicity and fame, Bauer received the 2010 National Media Excellence Award from the American Dietetic Association. As the founder and CEO of Joy Bauer Nutrition, she headed one of the largest nutrition centers in the country for close to two decades. She has been variously featured in prominent publications such as *The New York Times*, *Washington Post*, *Vogue*, and *The Wall Street Journal*, and has also authored 12 *New York Times* best-selling books.

As with Powell Jobs, these achievements should create a great philanthropist as well; yet it would be impossible to draw a line differentiating each individual's value and contribution, or the magnitude of their impact. Nevertheless, wealth remains an indicator where the difference can be plainly seen.

7 MARTHA INGRAM
B. AUGUST 20, 1935 (SOUTH CAROLINA, USA)

Martha Ingram is an American business executive and philan-thropist. In 1995, Martha Ingram succeeded her late husband as Chairman and CEO of Ingram Industries, one of America's largest privately-held companies. She married E. Bronson Ingram II, the son of business magnate Orrin Henry Ingram, Sr., on October 4, 1958.

H	D	M	Y
n/a	E 戊	T 甲	t 乙
n/a	W 辰	M 申	r 亥

BAZI SYSTEM · FOLLOW POWER

	16	26	36	46	56	66
LUCK CYCLE	F 丙	f 丁	E 戊	e 己	M 庚	m 辛
	H 戌	r 亥	R 子	g 丑	T 寅	t 卯

The Self has a fabulous energy system. As Yang Earth, she has three Wood elements clustered in a single area, forming a stellar Wood team. As Wood is her spouse element, this ensures a powerful and supportive spouse, which is nurtured further by the Water team of Dragon and Monkey. Although Ingram possesses a clear Follow Power system, it is also possible that she is following two providers - Power and Wealth - at the same time. In real terms, this could mean marrying a wealthy provider, as her life bears out. For males - and in modern times, career women also - the Power element represents an individual's career or boss. A prominent Power element within the chart denotes a successful career with all the trappings of wealth that go along with it.

Water and Wood are her beneficial elements, while Earth and Fire are detrimental. Coincidentally, Ingram Industries, being a giant book wholesaler, has exceptional Wood flow. Indeed, Ingram's power and wealth derive from publishing, a Wood industry, which is constantly nourishing and empowering her.

She gained a position in the company during a Rat period and in a Wood year, inheriting the wealth in her Tiger cycle, another Wood period. The Yin Metal which stripped her of a spouse, had the consequence of bestowing her fame instead. In fact, Ingram achieved fame after the death of her spouse, Yin Metal being the crucial fame element of a Yang Earth Self.

YEAR	AGE	LUCK CYCLE	KEY EVENTS
1957	22	Yin Fire, f丁	Worked at a radio and television station, owned by her father
1958	23	Dog, H戊	Married to the son of a business magnate
1979	44	Rat, R子	Director of Public Affairs at Ingram Industries
1995	60	Tiger, T寅	Chairman of the Board and CEO, ranked 524th on *Forbes'* list of richest people
2001	66	Yin Metal, m辛	Inducted into South Carolina Business Hall of Fame

Ronald Ernest "Ron" Paul, born on the same day in Pittsburgh, is an American physician, author, former Republican congressman and two-time Republican presidential candidate. He has enjoyed a successful and diversified career to match an impressive Bazi. We have included his luck cycle and key events for comparison.

LUCK CYCLE	24	34	44	54	64
	m辛	M庚	e己	E戊	f丁
	f巳	W辰	t卯	T寅	g丑

YEAR	AGE	LUCK CYCLE	KEY EVENTS
1971	36	Yang Metal, M庚	Entered politics
1976-1977	41-42	Dragon, W辰	Congressman
1979-1985	44-52	Rabbit, t卯	Congressman

Ron Paul's Wood and Water flows also led him into the medical field, as well as to various successes in the political arena. The table above shows how Water and Wood boosted his three monumental political victories.

8 CHRISTEL DEHAAN
B. OCTOBER 20, 1942 (NÖRDLINGEN, GERMANY)

Christel DeHaan is the founder and CEO of Christel House International. She co-founded Resort Condominiums International Inc. (RCI) in 1974, the world's largest vacation interval exchange company, becoming its chairman, CEO and sole shareholder in 1989. In November 1996, she sold RCI to HFS (now the Cendant Corporation) for 825 million dollars.

DeHaan has opened five "Christel House" schools, designed to provide an education to underprivileged children around the world. They are located in Bangalore, India; Mexico City, Mexico; Cape Town, South Africa; Caracas, Venezuela; and Indianapolis, Indiana, USA.

H	D	M	Y
n/a	F丙	M庚	R壬
n/a	F午	H戌	F午

BAZI SYSTEM · DOMINANT FIRE

LUCK CYCLE	13	23	33	43	53
	E戊	f丁	F丙	t乙	T甲
	M申	d未	F午	f巳	W辰

DeHaan is Yang Fire. Supported by a Fire team of the Horse and the Dog, she is Dominant Fire: bright, forward-looking, confident, energetic and goal-oriented. Fire, Wood and Earth are the beneficial elements, while Water is the most harmful. The Self is also one of the Intelligent Six, cosmically endowed with great intelligence.

YEAR	AGE	LUCK CYCLE	KEY EVENTS
1959-1961	17-19	Yang Earth, E戊	Administrative assistant in West Germany; married
1962	20	Monkey, M申	Moved to Indiana, USA; set up home business of typing and ironing
1973	31	Goat, d未	B.S. degree; remarried; developed real estate business with husband
1977-1989	35-47	Yang Fire Horse-Yin Wood, FF-t 丙午-乙	Business grew exponentially, becoming a leader of its industry

As her key events show, she thrives on real estate, riding on the exponential growth of a strong Fire flow during the ten years spanning ages 34 to 43. This was followed by 20 years of steady and strong Wood and Fire/Earth flow. In contrast, during the Monkey period (Water and Metal), Dehaan was encumbered by menial manual work in the United Kingdom.

Christiane Nüsslein-Volhard from Magdeburg, Germany, is a prominent biologist. She won the Albert Lasker Award for Basic Medical Research in 1991, and the Nobel Prize for Physiology in 1995, all in the Snake period of Fire and Earth. Between 1985 and 2008, from the ages of 43 to 66, the approximate 20 years of her Fire, Earth and Wood periods, she received 28 awards and over ten honorary degrees from global elite universities.

Nüsslein-Volhard is also a notable philanthropist. In 2004 she started the Christiane Nüsslein-Volhard Foundation to facilitate childcare for young mothers with promising careers in the field of science.

Both Dehaan and Nüsslein-Volhard were born in Germany, super-achievers dedicated to career and philanthropy, and interestingly, devoted to the welfare of children. The year 1991 was also a banner year for the two women; Dehaan was granted a divorce and became the independent investor and sole decision maker of her empire, while Nüsslein-Volhard won her first great award, paving the way for a host of further accolades.

Earl John Hindman, born in Bisbee, Arizona, was an American actor, best known for his recurring role as "Wilson", the unseen neighbor in television sitcom *Home Improvement*, which ran from 1991 to 1999. Prior to this, he played Bob Reid in *Ryan's Hope*, an American soap opera which aired for 13 years, featuring in 459 episodes spanning 1975 to 1989. A long-term smoker, Hindman's health ailed in 2003 and he died of lung cancer on December 29, 2003 in Connecticut.

The Fire from his acting career certainly benefited Hindman, with the prosperity from 1975 to 1989 comparable to Dehaan's period of exponential growth. They were both happily married in an equivalent time frame - 1977 to 1989 for Hindman vis-à-vis 1973 to 1991 for Dehaan. Yet why was Hindman saddled with a long-term smoking addiction that led to his premature death in 2003, while Dehaan continues to thrive?

Smokers normally have an inborn need for Fire support. Fire Selves, especially those with Dominant chart configurations, are so vulnerable to the attack of Water that many ultimately succumb to it. It seemed that Hindman had moved to the moist and cold northeast coast some time before he died, receiving little in the way of environmental support from Fire. He died in a wet month of a wet year - December 2003, year of the Yin Water Goat. Aged 61 at the time, Hindman was undergoing the Dragon period of his luck cycle, a challenging phase during which the Dragon clashed with the Dog in his month pillar, breaking down his Fire team.

DeHaan, on the other hand, has thrived ever since electing real estate as her business venture. Real estate, being an Earth industry according to Bazi classification, readily absorbs the Water, preventing it from engulfing her precious Fire. Earth also grants Fire Selves a mellow disposition: Dehaan is known for her grace and sophistication, yet has no desire to be in the public eye. She has also displayed great generosity to her many employees as well as the disadvantaged of the world. The good seeds thus sown tend to provide returning flows of cosmic protection.

Hindman did choose the right profession for attracting Fire flow. But why did he move to a cold and wet land? Clearly, with no knowledge of the finer workings of the Five Elements, this was not a cosmically-informed decision. On the other hand, one must remember that constant and focused hard work significantly strengthens our existing energy, invigorating the system and protecting us during down-cycles when the flow of energy typically stagnates and dwindles.

We currently have no data on the private life of Nüsslein-Volhard to illustrate how she coped during her own down-cycle, although there is little doubt that she is considered on all counts a fiercely focused hard worker. In Chinese metaphysics, a popular recipe for tiding over bad luck cycles is as follows: "Focus on hard work, study a difficult subject, stay on plain food and away from vices." It could explain why Nüsslein-Volhard, like Dehaan, has been able to reap the benefits of a smooth and successful life.

9 DONNA KARAN
B. OCTOBER 2, 1948 (NEW YORK, USA)

Donna Karan is one of the most influential fashion designers in the world, creating the Donna Karan New York and DKNY clothing labels. She has left a lasting impact on the world of fashion. In 2004, she received the Lifetime Achievement Award from the Council of Fashion Designers of America.

H	D	M	Y
n/a	M庚	m辛	E戊
n/a	M申	m酉	R子

BAZI SYSTEM · VARIABLE

	8	18	28	38	48
LUCK CYCLE	M庚	e己	E戊	f丁	F丙
	M申	d未	F午	f巳	W辰

The Self as Yang Metal, surrounded by a further three individual Metal elements, is a clear case of Sibling Rivalry.[4] She needs Fire to curtail her Siblings. Additional Metal signs (with the exception of an Ox or Snake) will also function like Siblings, posing stress and challenges. Wood, triggering the fight among the Metal Siblings, is equally undesirable.

Having said this, its configuration facilitates a Variable system: with the onset of an Ox or Snake, Karan could become powerful

---

4 Although there is a Monkey and a Rat in the branches, the Self cannot follow Water: The Rat is blocked from joining the Monkey by the Rooster - the flow of Metal is simply too powerful for the Rat to cross the barricade. It would require help from a Dragon or additional Rat/Monkey. The biggest trouble-maker, Monkey, has to turn to Water first.

Dominant Metal, while an additional Rat or Dragon, may render her a Follow Children type. Such variations, brought on by the changing flows of years or luck cycles, could well usher in great fortune. Let us see how these considerations have been borne out by her individual case history.

YEAR	AGE	LUCK CYCLE	KEY EVENTS
1951	3	...	Father died
1962-1967	14-19	Monkey, M申	Dropped out of school; sold clothing at local boutique store
1968-1973	20-25	Yin Earth, e己	Studied fashion design in New York City, working at Anne Klein during summer
1974	26	Goat, d未	Head designer at Anne Klein
1985	37	Horse, F午	Left Anne Klein and debuted her first women's collection
1988	40	Yin Fire, f丁	Launched DKNY, a women's line
1990-2000	42-52	Snake-Yang Fire, f-F巳-丙	Extended DKNY to jeans, menswear, children's clothes and furniture

YEAR	AGE	LUCK CYCLE	KEY EVENTS
2001	53	Dragon, W辰	Sold company to Moët Hennessy Louis Vuitton, a luxury French conglomerate, for close to $650 million
2003	55	Dragon, W辰	The first American to ever receive Fashion Group International's "Superstar Award"
2004	56	Dragon, W辰	Lifetime Achievement Award from the Council of Fashion Designers of America

As shown in the table above, Karan lost her father in the Metal and Wood year of 1951, the Yin Metal Rabbit. With the Ox setting in to join her Rooster making her a Dominant Metal Self in 1985, she succeeded in debuting her first women's collection. During her Snake five-year period, she became Dominant Metal once again, developing a host of products under the DKNY brand, which catered to all age groups and both genders.

The Dragon which joined the Rat and Monkey in her Bazi, brought her the best fortune. She received a number of awards and made a fortune on the sale of her company.

Persis Khambatta, also a member of the fashion circle elite, was an Indian model, actress, author and former Miss India. Below are her key life events for comparative discussion.

YEAR	AGE	LUCK CYCLE	KEY EVENTS
1950	2	...	Father deserted the family
1961	13	Yang Metal, M庚	First modeling job
1965	17	Monkey, M申	Won the Femina Miss India contest, and Miss Photogenic Award (Snake year)
1980	32	Yang Earth, E戊	Injured in car crash, Germany, leaving a scar to the head
1983	35	Horse, F午	Coronary bypass
1985	37	Horse, F午	Resumed career
1998	50	Yang Fire, F丙	Death from heart attack

Both Khambatta and Karan's birth systems revolve around the business of glamour, prospering on the sale of their talent and ideas. They lost their fathers in early childhood - aged two and three respectively - in years of strong Metal. With Metal and Wood as their dreaded elements, they also encountered setbacks from 1980 to 1984, periods of strong Metal and Wood. However, each responded in dramatically different ways.

Karan, anticipating a change, did two things: divorcing and quickly remarrying. At the same time, she planned to set up her own business in anticipation of an abrupt exit from the comfortable position she had hitherto enjoyed. Khambatta, on the other hand, reacted haphazardly to the unfavorable flows. Firstly, she was involved in a car crash in 1980, the year of the Yang Metal Monkey, sustaining an injury which left a scar to the head. She also underwent a coronary bypass in 1983, a powerful Wood year of the Yin Water Pig.

In 1985, an Ox showed up in the year: both women became Dominant Metal, poised for success. Karan launched her first Donna

Karan women's collection, while Khambatta reprised her career after recovering from the accident. Earlier, in 1965, whilst an unremarkable year for Karan, the Dominant Metal effect can be evidenced in Khambatta's case history, where the Snake paired with the Rooster in her month pillar, crowning her Miss India.

Khambatta passed away from a heart attack at age 49 in 1998, an inauspicious year in an otherwise good luck period: in this instance, the Tiger clashed with her health palace, the Monkey. She never made it to the best period that her system could offer, that is, the Dragon cycle from the age of 53. Karan, on the other hand, netted 650 million dollars on the sale of her company, reaping fortune and prosperity on an international scale.

Why the difference? Inherited genes, which determine one's capacity for good health and the ability to cope with challenge, are certainly fundamental. Likewise, the quality of each individuals' habitat as well as the culture of their societies (apparently in marked contrast, according to this example), surely plays an important role as well. While we cannot pinpoint or quantify their impact, attitude and personal choices are key.

§

From the foregoing nine discussions, we have witnessed how cosmic flows impact lives and shape destinies. While their impact is fundamental, it is, however, never decisive. The environment, physical or social, and crucially, our own personal choices, play a more defining role. Given the same birth energy, people raised or working in similar environments do tend to share more comparable life paths.

The samples in the chapters that follow will provide the greater degree of insight needed to draw a more meaningful conclusion.

CHAPTER SIX

DUPLICATE BIRTHS WITH DIVERGENT PATHS

This section covers the eight examples, along with their duplicate births, which show a greater degree of contrast in their achievements than those in the foregoing chapter. While their life paths are classified as divergent, naturally some traces of similarity remain.

§

1 UHURU KENYATTA
B. OCTOBER 26, 1961 (NAIROBI, KENYA)

Uhuru Kenyatta is the fourth President of Kenya. He is the son of Jomo Kenyatta, Kenya's founding father and first president.

H	D	M	Y
n/a	R壬	E戊	m辛
n/a	W辰	H戌	g丑

BAZI SYSTEM • FOLLOW POWER

	16	26	36	46	56
LUCK CYCLE	F丙	t乙	T甲	r癸	R壬
	M申	d未	F午	f巳	W辰

The Self is Yang Water. Born in a powerful Earth-Fire month and surrounded by four Earth elements, he is feeble Water - a great example of the Follow Power configuration. He favors Fire and Earth, dreading Wood and Water. Metal's effect could extend in either direction: while it has the negative consequence of empowering the Water, it also curtails Wood, protecting his Earth in the process.

During the Monkey period (a branch containing both Water and Metal) from the ages of 21 to 25, a patch of his life was given over to rumor and speculation, with no visible signs of progress or development. The 15 years of Wood flow from ages 26 to 40 are also mostly unaccounted for. Upon the onset of Fire at the age of 41, however, his political fortune abruptly surged, reaching its peak at 52 when he became President of Kenya.

How did Kenyatta become the deputy prime minister of Kenya during the Yin Water (r癸) period? Luckily, the would-be Sibling - Yin Water - was eliminated by an act of pairing with the Yang Earth (E戊) in his month stem.

YEAR	AGE	LUCK CYCLE	KEY EVENTS
Prior to 1997	<36	Wood	Studied political science at Amherst College, USA; exported agricultural produce after graduation
1999	38	Yang Wood, T甲	Chairman of the Kenya Tourism Board
2001-2002	40-41	Horse, F午	Minister for local government
2002-2007	41-46	Horse, F午	Party leader
2008-2013	47-52	Yin Water, r癸	Deputy Prime Minister of Kenya
Sep 2013	52	Snake, f巳	President

Dylan McDermott, from Connecticut, United States, is an actor with a very different career trajectory. Born to teenage parents who divorced when he was six years old, he was left in the care of his grandmother. During the Monkey cycle[1], he served drinks in his father's bar (Water). In contrast, Kenyatta, who hailed from a prominent family, was sent to the moist and freezing state of Massachusetts

---

1 Monkey, though categorized as a Metal branch, contains a substantial amount of Water. Indeed, there could be enough to function chiefly as a Water branch, since the Metal in the sign also serves the auxiliary function of empowering this Water. It would be helpful for readers and students to take responsibility for how each branch and stem works based on observation and experience, since Metaphysics is not a rigid science.

for study. The Water hurt both in different ways: while one toiled behind a bar, the other found himself relocated to a wet, coastal state far from the familiar comforts of home. Interestingly, they were close neighbors at the time.

Despite the fact that both are successful in their respective fields, what clearly emerges is that each suffered the negative impact of Wood flow from the ages of approximately 26 to 40. McDermott struggled with issues of alcohol abuse, while Kenyatta mysteriously kept this part of his life out of the public record.

What led to the key differences in their life paths? While it remains impossible to quantify their share of impact from DNA, upbringing, or physical, social, and political environments - as well as that of personal choice - two things stand out. Firstly, Kenyatta, coming from a caring and well-to-do family environment, undoubtedly holds the winning edge over the abandoned McDermott, whose mother died in tragic circumstances shortly after her divorce. Secondly, as a resident of an earthy, hot country, Kenyatta thrives on the abundant flow of Earth. With the backing of his natural environment, he enjoys cosmically-assisted success. In McDermott's lifetime, the Fire and Earth energy required for a comparable degree of success was never forthcoming due largely to the consistently cold and wet nature of his environs.

2 ELIZABETH HOLMES
B. FEBRUARY 3, 1984 (WASHINGTON, DC, USA)

Elizabeth Holmes was the founder and CEO of Theranos, a blood-testing company established in 2003. At the age of 31, she received *Forbes'* "Under 30 Doers" award, numbering among its "Youngest Power Women of 2015", as well as ranking in *Fortune*'s "Businessperson of the Year" list. By early 2016, however, Theranos was under investigation for fraud, as a result of which Holmes was promptly dropped from *Forbes'* billionaires list and her net worth ignominiously revised from 4.5 billion dollars to zero. The path took her from meteoric success story to abject failure in little over a decade, furnishing our investigation with its most dramatic depiction yet of the powerful impact of cosmic flows.

H	D	M	Y
n/a	f丁	t乙	r癸
n/a	t卯	g丑	r亥

BAZI SYSTEM · VARIABLE

	1	11	21	31
LUCK CYCLE	F丙	f丁	E戊	e己
	T寅	t卯	W辰	f巳

As a Yin Fire Self standing alone in the Bazi, supported by three Wood elements in a team and nurtured freely by natural rainwater, Holmes has a classic example of the Follow Resource configuration. She thrives on Wood and Water, dreading the Fire which disrupts her

Follow status, stripping her entitlement to protection and provision in the process.

However, this could also be a Variable system. How? She was born in a powerful Earth month, where the onset of additional strong Earth could confer Follow Children status. The fame and riches heaped liberally upon her prior to her downfall in 2016 indicate that Holmes' chart is indeed functioning as a Variable system. On all counts, Fire remains her most dreaded element.

She founded blood testing firm Theranos at the age of 19 in 2003, the year of the Yin Water Goat (rd癸未) - or in pictorial terms, Wood beneath rain. This occurred during the Rabbit period of her luck cycle, when the most powerful Wood trio was formed with the Pig and the Goat in her chart. The sky was the limit and swift success ensued.

At the age of 30 in 2014, a Horse year (TF甲午) taking place during the Dragon (W辰) luck cycle, she reached another crest in her career, establishing offices in every state of America. This time, the onset of the Dragon and Horse joined the Ox in her Bazi to form an Earth team, giving her Follow Children status. Theranos was valued at a staggering 9 billion dollars, catapulting Holmes into the *Forbes'* 400 list of 2014 and crowning her the world's youngest self-made female billionaire. Her "fame" luck continued to grow in early 2015 into her Yin Earth period, this being a great fame element of the Yin Fire Self.

However, cracks began to show in October 2015 (a Rooster month), as the powerful Metal launched an attack on her Wood provider, which punished the Self in turn when Theranos came under fire for fraud. In July 2016, as the Yang Fire of that year set in to destroy her Follow status, the Self was symbolically stripped of Wood's patronage, heavily penalized for the rebellion. Sanctions were imposed against Holmes and Theranos, prohibiting the ownership or operation of a lab for two years, and imposing a civil monetary penalty. Other lawsuits soon followed.

Being born on the cusp of two shifting flows, a shaky transitional period that fell on the last day of the lunar year, Holmes is subject to a very unstable, fluctuating energy; as such, she is fated to experience extreme peaks and troughs throughout her life.

YEAR	AGE	LUCK CYCLE	KEY EVENTS
2003	19	Rabbit, t 卯	Chemical engineering major at Stanford; founded Theranos
2014	30	Dragon, W 辰	Theranos licensed to operate in every US state; valued at $9 billion; youngest female billionaire on *Forbes'* 400 list; held 18 US patents
2015	31	Yin Earth, e 己	Ranked in *Fortune's* "Businessperson of the Year" and *Forbes'* "Youngest Power Women of 2015"; received *Forbes'* "Under 30 Doers" Award
Oct 2015	32	Yin Earth, e 己	Theranos investigated
Jul 2016	33	Yin Earth, e 己	Sanctions from the Medicare and Medicaid Services, a Yang Fire Monkey year (FM, 丙申)

In contrast to Holmes, **Sara Carbonero** did not choose the medical field to enhance her Wood flow - instead, as a sports journalist, she burns the Wood into Fire to support her profession, which by cosmic definition, belongs to the domain of Fire. In other words, she is constantly draining Wood resources in order to sustain her livelihood. Despite the limited information we have on her life, the trajectory of her career appears muted when compared to that of Holmes, and certainly far less dramatic. Holmes, who established her company in Palo Alto, is supported by an area bountiful in old trees and part of the moist Bay Area. This intensely wooded area reinforces the cosmic energy of Water and Wood that she requires to succeed.

What can account for such variation despite the similarities in cosmic energy? In particular, how do we explain Holmes' rapid and phenomenal success? To begin with, Holmes seems to have inherited a daring and inventive streak from her great-great-grandfather, Christian R. Holmes, who was a surgeon, engineer, and inventor. He also inspired her to study medicine which, by natural Bazi classification, comprises Wood and Water, bountiful in her cosmic chart. It remains for us to speculate whether her intrepid spirit, springing from Viking-Danish DNA, may indeed have inspired the bold and risky decisions which brought about those dazzling gains, as well as such a startling fall from grace.

3 JEFFREY BEZOS
B. JANUARY 12, 1964 (NEW MEXICO, USA)

Jeffrey Bezos is an American technology entrepreneur who has played a significant role in the growth of e-commerce worldwide. He is the founder and CEO of Amazon.com, initially an online marketplace for books which later expanded to supply a wide range of products.

In 2015, Amazon.com became the largest retailer on the web and a model of internet sales, surpassing Walmart as the United States' most valuable retailer. Bezos bought *The Washington Post* in 2013, and went on to acquire Wholefoods in 2017. In March 2018, he became the richest man in the world (*Forbes*).

H	D	M	Y
n/a	M庚	t乙	r癸
n/a	M申	g丑	t卯

BAZI SYSTEM · VARIABLE

	22	32	42	52	62
LUCK CYCLE	R壬	m辛	M庚	e己	E戊
	H戌	m酉	M申	d未	F午

The Self is Yang Metal. Supported by a Metal house (Ox, g丑) and another Yang Metal (the Monkey, M申) in the day branch, he is a Strong Metal Self. At first glance, his system could easily be classified as one of Sibling Rivalry, with all the challenges that go along with it. Fortunately, the Self has the advantage of being the constant winner in Sibling combat due to the presence of other Metal signs (his symbolic Siblings) hidden in the branches.

Having said that, the system is too changeable and versatile to fall into any rigid classification; it is indeed a classic Variable type. Let us sort through the potential to see how it works in real time.

Firstly, the onset of a Rooster or Snake will transform him into a Dominant Metal Self, powerful enough to take charge of all the Wood financial resources coming his way, and bestowing quick riches. This scenario can take place during any Snake or Rooster hour, day, month, or year, as well as at any time that a Snake or Rooster may be found in his luck period. How does this flow translate into practice?

During his Rooster period from the ages of 37 to 41 (2001 to 2005), Bezos became a Dominant Metal Self. The hard work of diversification and restructuring that had taken place since 1998 was finally paying dividends and, in 2003, Amazon had begun to turn a profit of some 400 million dollars, a significant development. In 2005, a Rooster year within the Rooster luck cycle, Amazon reached another milestone, entering the video streaming and rental business for the first time.

In 2013 (ef癸巳), a Snake year, an exciting breakthrough saw Bezos secure a 600 million-dollar contract with the Central Intelligence Agency (CIA) on behalf of Amazon Web Services. Bezos declared that he would never have to drive a truck again. During the latter part of that year, in October, Amazon was announced the largest online shopping retailer worldwide.

Yet another Rooster impact took place during the Fire Rooster year of 2017 (fm丁酉), when his grand design for the building of three interconnected biodomes finally manifested in the form of the Amazon Spheres in Seattle, Washington State.

Construction of Amazon's headquarters in Seattle had begun in the Wood year of 2015 (td乙未). The structure comprises three domed conservatories, home to more than 40,000 plants from the cloud forest regions of over 30 countries, a vast concentration of Wood resources from which Bezos can tap his vast wealth. There are 40 to 50 trees in the spheres, the largest being 55 feet tall (17 metres). These plants are housed within ambient domes whose temperature and humidity are carefully monitored day and night.

Their completion took place on January 29, 2018[2], a pure Metal day in a Water-Metal month and a Metal year, all the more impressive when we consider that such a day is auspiciously designated for

Successful Completion[3] according to the Chinese Almanac. It would be difficult to speculate how the idea for this unique project came about - what we do know is that consciously or otherwise, Bezos seems to be well attuned with the Bazi

H	D	M	Y
n/a	m 辛	r 癸	f 丁
n/a	m 酉	g 丑	m 酉

JANUARY 29, 2018

principles governing his birth system, acting in close alignment with the beneficial elements that grant him such ready success.

The phenomenal Rooster year of 2017 also saw Amazon stock surge to a ten-year high, as a result of which Bezos was ranked the richest man in the world in early 2018 during a powerful Wood month, reflecting the dynamic effects of Metal and Wood working in tandem.

Secondly, the onset of a Dragon, a Rat, or both, could join forces with the Monkey to create an alliance of Water, effectively eliminating the Yang Metal Sibling and diluting the Ox's Earth energy in the process, placing the Self into a Follow configuration. The powerful Water, besides polishing the Self, would then empower the Wood, making the Self both Follow Children and Follow Wealth.

---

2 N.B. The Fire Rooster year officially ended on February 3, 2018.
3 The Chinese Almanac grouped all calendars days into 12 categories by the 12 branches in the lunar calendar. Each category has a different nature, serving different functions. While a few are particularly auspicious, some must be avoided by all means possible when performing important tasks. The nature of each day changes over the years depending on the cosmic flow cycle. November 1, 1994, the day that Bezos registered "Amazon" as his company name, was a *Grasping* day, meaning steadily holding-up and marching-on. The top three auspicious days are: *Successful Completion*, *Grasping*, and *Opening*. Bezos landed two of them for his key ventures.

This process happened twice in Bezos's life, and they turned out to be his most auspicious periods. In 2008, a Rat year, he was rated by *U.S. News & World Report* as one of America's best leaders, the same year that he was also awarded an honorary doctorate in science and technology from Carnegie Mellon University. The Rat joined the Monkey to form a Water team, eliminating the Yang Metal hidden in the Monkey, which transformed his Bazi into a Follow Children configuration.

The Dragon year of 2012 earned Bezos the titles of "Businessperson of The Year" by *Fortune*, and "Second Best CEO in the World" by *Harvard Business Review*. In forming an alliance with the Monkey, the Dragon achieved the same result as did the Rat four years earlier. In this instance the Water pillar of 2012, being so much more powerful, held the potential to create a great deal more wealth than had previously been possible.

What's more, since Wood is his fundamental source of wealth and already in rich supply in his Bazi, the onset of any additional Wood could easily create a more potent form of the Follow Wealth system. Let us trace some of his key events to show the impact of Wood on his life. In the Yin Earth Rabbit year of 1999 (et己卯), Bezos became *TIME* magazine's "Person of the Year". Wood flow also inspired him to innovate the Amazon Kindle in 2007 (fr丁亥), for which he won an innovation award from the *Economist* in the Wood-rich year of 2011 (mt辛卯). What of the company name itself? Remarkably, Bezos seems to have landed haphazardly on the most cosmically-fortunate name that he could have chosen.

His biography tells us that he had always been drawn to the letter "A" given that he wanted to stake his claim at the top of most website listings, which were arranged alphabetically at the time. Interestingly, however, Bezos had established the company in April 1994 under a different name. It was not until later that the fortunate decision was made to change it, the new name being registered on November 1, 1994. While the Wood flow from 1994 (TH甲戌) certainly pushed him headlong into the book-selling business, he had to bide his time for the emergence of additional Wood flow, first from November, a month particularly rich in Wood, then from the day itself, being one of strong Wood-Metal flow from the Yin Wood Rabbit (tm 辛 卯), before inspiration endowed him with this perfect metaphor. How is this significant? The Amazon, Earth's largest river, supplying the world's largest rainforest, represents a vast body of Water with which to nurture the Wood that cosmically functions as his wealth base, and by extension, the books he sells online. Bezos' wealth element, Wood - symbolically, the Amazon jungle, and later, the private jungle of his Amazon spheres - effectively becomes his unlimited source of wealth.

Having a Variable Bazi configuration can only account for so much of his fortune. His system also benefits from several other features, all of which confer wealth and protection. As a Yang Metal Self, his money sign is the Yin Wood (t 乙) which naturally pairs up with the Yang Metal (M 庚) Self.[4] Furthermore, there are two such money signs in his chart, each volunteering to pair with the Self. What are the implications? Literally, it means money falling into his pocket from multiple streams of revenue.

Furthermore, as both the *Yang* and *Yin Guard*[5] protect from dangers or evil, he is always rewarded for the boldness of his ventures, no matter how creative or risky they seem - a sure measure of success.

One final feature of his system warrants discussion: there is a *Crossing-Resource* between the month and the day pillars. The Monkey, with its Water, is the resource of the Yin Wood; the Ox, with its Earth is the resource of the Yang Metal, keeping apace with the growing financial resources. It signifies a crisscrossing of support to the Self from various sources, an extremely rare and fortunate development.

---

4 See Chapter Three for Stem Pairing.
5 See *Fig. 3g*, Chapter Three.

YEAR	AGE	LUCK CYCLE	KEY EVENTS
1986	22	Yang Water, R壬	At Princeton University studying computer and electrical engineering
1994	30	Dog, H戌	Founded Amazon.com, originally named Cadabra
Oct 1994	30	Dog, H戌	Changed company name to Amazon
1999	35	Yin Metal, m辛	*TIME* "Person of the Year"
2008	44	Yang Metal, M庚	Named one of America's best leaders in *U.S. News & World Report*
2011	47	Monkey, M申	Innovation Award for Amazon Kindle from *The Economist*
2012	48	Monkey, M申	"Businessperson of The Year" by *Fortune*; 26th on The World's Billionaires list (*Forbes*); "Second Best CEO in the World" by *Harvard Business Review*
2015	51	Monkey, M申	Construction of Amazon Spheres in Seattle
Jan 30, 2018	54	Yin Earth, e己	Opening of Amazon Spheres for employees
Mar 2018	54	Yin Earth, e己	Richest man in the world (*Forbes*)

John Seru leads a different destiny. As an actor, he also owns a wrestling school, fitness center and fitness shop, which he has been running for 18 years in Sydney with his family.

Born and raised in Fiji, we know little about his family and education. Growing up in an isolated island state, a predominantly farming region, he certainly was not connected to the elite culture of Princeton or high tech businesses by any means. Instead, he was trained at the Malenko Wrestling Academy in Tampa, Florida, and ran his own wrestling gym for 10 years before entering the acting industry.

He does, however, share a couple of the same banner years as Bezos. As an actor, he is known for *The World Is Not Enough* (1999) and *Do or Die* (2001).

4 PRINCE AL-WALEED BIN TALAL
B. MARCH 7, 1955 (JEDDAH, SAUDI ARABIA)

Prince Al-Waleed bin Talal bin Abdulaziz al Saud, a member of the Saudi royal family, is a Saudi business magnate and investor. He is the founder, CEO and chief owner of the Kingdom Holding Company.

H	D	M	Y
n/a	f丁	e己	t乙
n/a	t卯	t卯	d未

BAZI SYSTEM · FOLLOW RESOURCE

LUCK CYCLE	21	31	41	51	61
	F丙	t乙	T甲	r癸	R壬
	R子	r亥	H戌	m酉	M申

The Self as Yin Fire is supported by a powerful Wood team all the way from the year pillar to the day branch - a beautiful Follow Resource system, typically belonging to those who are intelligent, gentle, congenial, and shrewd enough to bring about enormous life-long success. He craves Wood and Water, and dreads Metal and Fire.

The Yang Fire period from ages 21 to 25 posed some setbacks, delaying his college education. In fact, the prince did not graduate from Syracuse University until the age of 30, the final year of his Rat Water period. With Water assisting throughout his college years, he graduated with honors.

The effect of Wood, however, was more miraculous. In 1991, the Goat year reinforced his existing Wood alliance, and he bought shares in Citicorp, turning an initial investment of 550 million dollars into 1 billion dollars. In 2011 (mt辛卯), the Rabbit elevated his Wood alliance into a full trio, and his 300 million-dollar investment into Twitter was valued at 8 billion dollars by late summer of that year.

Water also contributed to his good fortune. In 2008, a Rat year taking place during his Yin Water period, he was listed as one of *TIME* magazine's 100 most influential people in the world, with an estimated net worth of 28 billion dollars. In 2015, he was ranked at 34 of *Forbes'* richest men in the world.

It seems astonishing that an individual clearly thriving on Wood and Water energy can prosper so phenomenally in an arid region such as the Middle East. On closer inspection, however, we see that the Prince was born in Jeddah, the largest sea port on the Red Sea, an important commercial hub in Saudi Arabia, with an abundant flow of Water to support the Wood he needs. Being one of Saudi Arabia's primary resort cities, it will also be well developed with Water resources and flora for tourism. In addition, the Prince loves yachting; he owns the 65th largest private yacht in the world.

We do not have enough data on the years during his Rooster period to account for the impact of Metal. The fortunate developments of 2015 (see table below) in the last leg of his Rooster period, seems to have been attributed to a strong flow of Wood from that year. One dramatic event, however, did take place in November 2017, a Metal month within a Rooster year, which certainly affords us some insights.

The prince was arrested in Saudi Arabia and detained at the Ritz-Carlton hotel in Riyadh with several other prominent Saudis on charges including money laundering, bribery, and extortion. He was released following a financial settlement on January 27, 2018, a Yin Earth Goat day, after a detention period of nearly three months. The Goat clashed away the final traces of Metal hidden in the Ox. Prior to this event, the aging Saudi King had made the unprecedented move of naming his son as heir to the throne, rather than following time-honored rules of royal succession which passes the crown from brother to brother within the same generation.

In the powerful Earth year of 2018 (EH戊戌), the prince suffered a significant setback when he was dropped from *Forbes'* Billionaires list as a corollary of the aforementioned anti-corruption initiative. His Wood flow was being deprived of support from Water.

YEAR	AGE	LUCK CYCLE	KEY EVENTS
1985	30	Rat, R子	Master's degree in social science from Syracuse University
1991	36	Pig, r亥	Bought substantial shares in Citicorp, turning $550 million into $1 billion
2008	53	Yin Water, r癸	Listed as one of *TIME* magazine's 100 most influential people in the world; estimated net worth of $28 billion
2011	56	Yin Water, r癸	Made $8 billion from an investment of $300 million in Twitter
2015	60	Rooster, m酉	*Forbes* listed Al-Waleed as the 34th richest man in the world, with an estimated net worth of $28 billion
Nov 4, 2017	62	Yang Water, R壬	Arrested in Saudi Arabia, in anti-corruption purge

YEAR	AGE	LUCK CYCLE	KEY EVENTS
Jan 27, 2018	62	Yang Water, R壬	Released from detention following a financial settlement after nearly three months detention
Mar 2018	63	Yang Water, R壬	Dropped out from *Forbes'* Billionaires' list

Tommy Kramer, a distinguished former football quarterback from San Antonio, Texas, United States, chose another field in which to flourish.

His habitat is not quite as dry as that of the Middle East, and he also operates within a vastly different social environment. Following the lead of his high school talents, he was inducted into the College Football Hall of Fame in 2012, a watery year of the Dragon (RW壬辰), for his standout collegiate career at Rice. Apparently a leader in the field of sports, as his Bazi potential indicates, he also enjoys the benefits of Water. Personal choice and environment truly make a difference to our destiny.

5 CHARLES ERGEN
B. MARCH 1, 1953 (TENNESSEE, USA)

Charles Ergen is an American businessman, the co-founder, current board chairman, and former CEO of Dish Network and EchoStar Communications Corporation. He stepped down as CEO in May 2011, remaining chairman of the board of both companies.

H	D	M	Y
n/a	m辛	T甲	r癸
n/a	r亥	T寅	f巳

BAZI SYSTEM · VARIABLE

	18	28	38	48	58	68
LUCK CYCLE	R壬	m辛	M庚	e己	E戊	f丁
	R子	r亥	H戌	m酉	M申	d未

The Self is Yin Metal born in the spring when Wood dominates. There are three Wood elements (one hidden in the Pig) empowered by rain (Yin Water), so Wood becomes the dominant flow. The Self has a shaky Follow Wealth system as the Snake in the year branch clashes with the Pig in the day branch. A special mechanism is required to transform the Snake, in order to convert his chart into a stable Follow Wealth system. This took place in 1998, a Tiger year during his Dog period; the Tiger and Dog clubbed together to form a Fire alliance, destroying the Metal contained within the Snake. It was at this point that Ergen entered the club of *Forbes'* 400 richest men. As a Follow Wealth type, the Metal Self benefits most from an unimpeded flow of Wood; the onset of a Goat or a Rabbit, forming a Wood alliance with his Pig, would increase his financial gains.

On the other hand, whenever the Snake is joined by either the Ox or the Rooster, it transforms into a Metal team, rendering him Dominant Metal. With hard work, he could dominate the field. Indeed, during his Rooster period, Ergen became the recipient of many awards and worked hard to complete the acquisitions which led to the expansion of his empire.

At other times, he is a weak Metal Self enjoying the assistance of additional Metal to exploit his rich reserves of Wood. During his Yin and Yang Metal periods - that is, the figurative arrival of more weapons with which to chop the Wood wealth - he was able to push his company to further expansion. The additional energy was a welcome development, bolstering the effort needed to succeed. Ergen's Variable system is one which creates versatile and tenacious individuals, who thrive in changing environments and professions.

YEAR	AGE	LUCK CYCLE	KEY EVENTS
...	Early 20s	Yang Water, R壬	Studied finance at the University of Tennessee; became a CPA
1980	27	Rat, R子	Founded EchoStar with wife and friend; sold satellite dishes door-to-door (Colorado)
1990	37	Yin Metal, m辛	Pushed EchoStar into the big leagues by raising $335 million in junk bonds and purchasing satellite orbital slots

YEAR	AGE	LUCK CYCLE	KEY EVENTS
1993	40	Yang Metal, M庚	EchoStar was incorporated; net income doubled to $20.4 million
1998	45	Dog, H戌	*Forbes'* 400 richest
2001	48	Yin Earth, e己	Frost & Sullivan, CEO of the Year of Satellite Industry
2007	54	Rooster, m酉	One of the "World's Best CEOs" by *Barron's* magazine
2007-2011	54-58	Rooster, m酉	Completed several acquisitions

Renate Blauel is a German music producer and sound engineer, thriving on Metal.

M. K. Stalin is an Indian politician who was deputy chief minister of Tamil Nadu from 2009 to 2011. He landed the position during the Ox year of his Rooster period, when he became Dominant Metal.

Carlos Queiroz was a football goalkeeper in Mozambique. He moved to Portugal following Mozambique's independence in 1975, and became a manager of Portugal's national football team. He seems to have benefited from the strong Wood flow of 1975 (tt乙卯) which led to the start of his career in Portugal.

Chuck Sito is an American actor, amateur boxer, celebrity bodyguard, stuntman, former boxing trainer, and former president of the New York chapter of the Hells Angels. He has been able to capitalize on his various talents to launch different careers at appropriate times.

6 JAYSHREE ULLAL
B. MARCH 27, 1961 (LONDON, ENGLAND)

Jayshree Ullal, a resident of the San Francisco Bay Area, is currently President and CEO of Arista Networks, a cloud networking company. She was born in London, but raised and educated in New Delhi, India, going on to obtain a bachelor's degree in electrical engineering from San Francisco State University, and a master's degree in engineering management from Santa Clara University.

H	D	M	Y
n/a	e己	m辛	m辛
n/a	d未	t卯	g丑

BAZI SYSTEM · FOLLOW POWER

	3	13	23	33	43	53
LUCK CYCLE	R壬	r癸	T甲	t乙	F丙	f丁
	W辰	f巳	F午	d未	M申	m酉

The Self is Yin Earth, being extremely intelligent on two counts. First, possessing a Yin Earth Goat day pillar, she is one of the Intelligent Six. Second, she is moist Earth enfeebled by a Wood team and three Yin Metal elements (m辛), making her a Follow type that adheres to the two leading flows of Wood and Metal. Follow Selves are, by classification, extremely intelligent, observant, alert, versatile, and pleasing to work with.

However, as Wood and Metal are in conflict, one element must take the lead. In this case, Wood has the upper hand since it enjoys the support of a team and benefits from good timing, thriving in the spring. As her life events indicate, she blossomed with the onset of Wood flows, managing to succeed exponentially in the Yang Fire period which served to quietly eliminate the Yin Metals, clearing a path for Wood to take full charge. The onset of a Rabbit (Wood) in 2011 also lifted her to new crests, when she was named in *Forbes* as "one of the top five most influential people in the networking industry today." Ullal falls into a Follow Power chart configuration, a highly intelligent, intuitive individual.

The most dreaded element is the Earth which disrupts her Follow Power status; it occurred in her late childhood from the ages of 8 to 12 when she was uprooted from London to India. Being under the care of her parents, however, this was a relatively harmless development.

Her career development is summed up in the following table:

YEAR	AGE	LUCK CYCLE	KEY EVENTS
1988	27	Yang Wood, T甲	Vice president of marketing at Crescendo
1993	32	Horse, F午	Oversaw 20 acquisitions for Cisco in 15 years; promoted to Senior Vice President of Data Center and Switching.
2011	47	Yin Fire, f丁	CEO and President of Arista Networks, a cloud networking company in Santa Clara, CA
2014	53	Yin Fire, f丁	Put Arista Networks on the New York Stock Exchange as ANET
2015	54	Yin Fire, f丁	One of America's richest self-made women

YEAR	AGE	LUCK CYCLE	KEY EVENTS
2016	55	Yin Fire, f丁	Arista ranked #2 on *Forbes'* list of fast track top 25 profitable tech companies

Six other notable individuals were born on the same date, all male. Being male, their luck cycle is reversed, and unfortunately, a prime period in their lives, roughly from the ages of 17 to 31, is plagued with Earth, the most detrimental element impacting their achievements. The great Earth Dog period from ages 57 to 66 is also particularly harmful.

In marked contrast, Ulall, being female, was fortunate enough to escape the Earth periods in the prime window of her life, gliding with the good flows to enjoy success and prosperity.

Here is the luck cycle of her male counterparts for reference:

LUCK CYCLE	17	27	37	47	57
	e己	E戊	f丁	F丙	t乙
	g丑	R子	r亥	H戌	m酉

The example closest to Ullal's successful career arc is that of **Valerijs Kargin**, a Latvian economist and banker. Demonstrating the same entrepreneurial and executive skills, albeit in a different enterprise, Kargin was the first to create a currency exchange corporation and open one of the first travel agencies in the Soviet Union during 1991.

He went on to become the president and chairman of Parex Banka from 1998 to 2008 (between the ages of 37 to 47) during the Yin Fire and Pig period, a fortuitous result of Yin Fire's control of the Metal elements, as well as the Pig's ability to form a Wood trio thereafter. Over the next five years of Yang Fire from the age of 47, he remained

Chairman: the Yang Fire naturally eliminated the destructive Yin Metal, making him a faithful Follow Power.

Mark Francis Cohen is a former Irish cricketer. His memorable years, 1987 (ft丁卯) and 1994 (TH甲戌), all comprise Wood years mixed with Fire. Naturally, he opted for a career involving much time spent on the lawn to bolster his Wood flow, although his time in the spotlight ended with the approach of the Earth period.

Nikita Borisovich Dzhigurda is a famous Russian actor, singer, and cult media icon. The Wood impact also showed in his career, particularly during the Pig year of 2007 (fr丁亥), his most productive to date and one in which he produced three films. Other periods of heightened productivity can be seen taking place during Wood or Water years.

Takahiro "Tak" Matsumoto, born in Osaka, Japan, is a Grammy Award-winning Japanese guitarist, producer, composer, singer and songwriter. In addition to being the guitarist and lead composer for the hard rock duo B'z, he has also enjoyed a successful solo career. During the Pig year of 2007, the two-man group became the first Asian band to be inducted into Hollywood's Rock Walk of Fame. In the Metal Rabbit year of 2011, he was ranked first in a poll on whom the Japanese people considered the best guitarist to represent Japan.

Tony Rominger, born in Vejle, Denmark, is a Swiss former professional road racing cyclist who won the Vuelta a España in 1992 (RM壬申), 1993 (rm癸酉), and 1994 (TH甲戌), and the Giro d'Italia in 1995 (tr乙亥), these being Wood or Water years.

Marcelo Daniel Colombo, born in Buenos Aires, Argentina, is a prelate of the Roman Catholic Church who has been serving as bishop of La Rioja since 2013 from the age of 52 during the Fire periods.

7 ABDELAZIZ BOUTEFLIKA
B. MARCH 2, 1937 (OUJDA, MOROCCO)

Abdelaziz Bouteflika is the fifth president of Algeria, having been appointed to the post in 1999. Prior to this, he was the minister of foreign affairs from 1963 to 1979. As President, he presided over the end of the bloody Algerian Civil War in 2002, ending emergency rule in February 2011 amid regional unrest.

H	D	M	Y
n/a	E戊	R壬	f丁
n/a	R子	T寅	g丑

BAZI SYSTEM · WEAK SELF

	19	29	39	49	59	69
LUCK CYCLE	M庚	e己	E戊	f丁	F丙	t乙
	R子	r亥	H戌	m酉	M申	d未

The Self is Yang Earth born in an early spring. To simplify our analysis process, we can ignore the effects of stems R壬 and f丁, as they mostly offset each other by pairing.

Being weakened by the penetrating roots sprouting from the thriving springtime Wood, together with the Earth-diluting Water directly beneath the Self, he is weak Earth. Yet, his enfeeblement is not absolute - there is Earth hidden in both the Tiger and Ox, reinforcing the Self and preventing him from becoming a Follow type. He benefits, therefore, from Fire and additional Earth, whilst dreading Water, Wood and Metal.

Typically, Bouteflika has struggled to make political headway during his Water and Wood periods. He was only able to gain a stable foothold in office shortly before the big Earth (E戊) period, when the upcoming support of Earth bolstered his weak Self. He continued to progress over the next few Earth years. During the Dog (H戌) period, with the solid support of Fire and Earth it contained, he was able to glide with relative ease over the mishaps brought on by the intervening years of powerful Metal in 1981 and Wood flow in 1983, when he was sued for having stolen the Algerian embassies' money between 1965 and 1979. Despite the hefty fines levied, he managed to sit tight on his established position. With the onset of empowering Yang Fire at 62, Bouteflika became President of Algeria.

From 2005 to 2014, however, in the wake of additional Wood, Metal and Water, which significantly debilitated his Earth flow, Bouteflika endured chronic hospitalizations.

YEAR	AGE	LUCK CYCLE	KEY EVENTS
1963	26	Rat, R子	Minister for Foreign Affairs
1974	37	Pig, r亥	Additional post, President of the United Nations General Assembly
1981	44	Dog, H戌	In 1981 (mm辛酉), he was sued for having stolen Algerian embassies' money between 1965 and 1979
1983	46	Dog, H戌	A powerful year of rr癸亥 sees him convicted and fined a hefty sum
1999	62	Yang Fire, F丙	President of Algeria, the longest serving president

YEAR	AGE	LUCK CYCLE	KEY EVENTS
2005-2014	68-77	Monkey to Goat, M-d 申-未	Several hospitalizations

Alfred "Alf" Jones was not so fortunate. Being an English professional footballer, he stayed in the club for just a few years before ending up a car factory worker in England. He did manage to play in non-league football later, without making significant contributions.

Why the difference? Amongst the many variables, the factor of environment seems to stand out. While Bouteflika is supported by the hot dry climate of Algeria, Jones' energy has been dissipated by the moist and cold nature of English weather, most unwelcome in a chart that depends on the flow of strong Earth and Fire.

8 SIR ARTHUR ALEXANDER FOULKES
B. MAY 11, 1928 (MATTHEW TOWN, BAHAMAS)

Arthur Foulkes was Governor-General of the Bahamas from 2010 to 2014.

H	D	M	Y
n/a	m辛	f丁	E戊
n/a	r亥	f巳	W辰

BAZI SYSTEM · VARIABLE

	28	38	48	58	68	78
LUCK CYCLE	M庚	m辛	R壬	r癸	T甲	t乙
	M申	m酉	H戌	r亥	R子	g丑

The Self is Yin Metal born in a Snake month. He is strong and has the opportunity to become Dominant whenever the Ox or Rooster comes along. However, there is too much Earth concealing it - the Metal is scarcely given a chance to shine. On the other hand, with so much of the Resource element Earth nurturing the Metal, in very rare circumstances, he could transform into Follow Resource, enjoying quick though fleeting success. Foulkes' chart can be classed as a Variable system depending on the input of external flows.

In fact, the conversion to Follow Resource did take place once in his lifetime, when he earned a position in the House of Assembly at the age of 54. The year was 1982, an earthy Dog year fortuitously set within his Dog period, when a double dose of Earth entered his system.

As a rule, however, he tends to benefit chiefly from the Wood element, this being used to curtail the strength of Earth. Before the age of 34, Foulkes struggled to achieve anything meaningful in terms of career. With the advent of a Monkey to dilute Earth's potency at age 34, however, he became the founding editor of a newspaper. At 40, following the growing momentum of Metal flow, he entered politics. Finally at 44, during the Rooster (Metal) period, he became Dominant Metal, landing a seat in the Senate.

At 64, as the Pig from his luck cycle teamed up with the Pig in his birth chart, he became the high commissioner to the United Kingdom, as well as ambassador to France, Germany, Italy, Belgium, Cuba and China. The strong Wood finally came to his rescue, keeping the Earth at bay. In the Yin Wood period, he became the governor-general of the Bahamas.

YEAR	AGE	LUCK CYCLE	KEY EVENTS
1962-1967	34-39	Monkey, M 申	Founding editor of *Bahamian Times*, the official paper of the Progressive Liberal Party
1968	40	Yin Metal, m 辛	Minister of Communications, then Minister of Tourism
1972-1977	44-49	Rooster, m 酉	Senate
1982	54	Dog, H 戌	House of Assembly
1992-1999	64-71	Pig, r 亥	Bahamas' High Commissioner to the United Kingdom; ambassador to France, Germany, Italy, Belgium, Cuba and China
2010-2014	82-86	Yin Wood, t 乙	Governor-General of the Bahamas

Yaacov Agam, an Israeli artist, found a remarkable way to alleviate the burden of troublesome Earth. As an experimental artist, best known for his contributions to optical and kinetic art, his sculptural creations utilize Earth energy, draining and dissipating it. As shown in the table below, he succeeded particularly during flows of Metal and Wood.

YEAR	AGE	LUCK CYCLE	KEY EVENTS
1953-1967	25-39	Mostly Metal	Began to exhibit, lecturing on experimental arts; gaining visibility
1974-1989	40s-61	Rooster to Yin Water, m-r 酉·癸	Global recognition, awards in 1974, 1977, 1985, 1989; honorary Ph.D. in 1975 from various institutes
1996	68	Pig, r 亥	Jan Amos Comenius Medal from UNESCO for "device on effective visual teaching for children"
2009	81	Yin Wood, t 乙	*4 Themes Contrepoint* was sold for $326,500
2010	82	Yin Wood, t 乙	*Growth*, an outsize kinetic painting done in oil on a wood panel, was sold for the record-breaking sum of $698,000

Both Foulkes and Agam benefit from Wood and Metal's ability to curtail the excessive amounts of Earth in their chart. However, their chosen careers diverge into entirely different fields: Foulkes in printing with machine and paper, Agam in art, with a particular emphasis on sculpture, working with media of fiber and wood. Both enjoyed a breakthrough in 1968, and continued to succeed. Similarly, their banner years are dominated by Metal and Wood. The two historical sales of Agam's artwork were completed during a period which benefited from the full range of Wood, or both Wood and Metal working hand in hand.

§

These examples demonstrate the breadth of diversification possible amongst those sharing the same cosmic energy flow. Yet, notwithstanding the impact of our physical and social environments, or the vagaries of personal choice, it is clear that the fundamental current of our cosmic energy remains constant as a presiding force. The variety of stories covered between the foregoing two chapters have surely demonstrated the many complexities of Bazi study.

CHAPTER SEVEN

MODERN CHINESE BILLIONAIRES

C hina has an extensive roll call of modern billionaires, offering
fertile ground for the study of Bazi. The revelatory nature of
one's Bazi, however, means that not many Chinese will be comfortable disclosing their full birth data, listing only the year to satisfy corporate requirements. We were fortunate, then, to find 13 individuals
among *Forbes'* 100 richest Chinese billionaires of 2015, whose birth
data includes the birth year, month and day.

The richest person in China of that year, Wang Jianlin, is a special
case which has already been used as an illustration in Chapter Four.
Two of the 13 were eliminated on the basis that there are insufficient
public records with which to furnish discussion. That leaves the remaining 10 to be examined in the current chapter.

Who are these billionaires? All are male, with the exception of a
single female whose husband also happens to be a co-founder of her
firm. They are relatively young, born between 1964 and 1971, with
the majority of birthdays falling within the mid-1960s. Each of them
succeeded at a remarkably early age, six having built their companies before the age of 30, two at 31, and another two at 32 and 37.
Significantly, all are self-made billionaires.

Did cosmic flow play a role in these outcomes? By metaphysical
law, we are in the eighth Feng Shui period which favors innovations
relating to fingers (keyboard work), the Earth (property), and the

achievements of young males on all fronts. Undoubtedly, the cosmic energy systems of this exceptional group are fabulously auspicious. We will cover the roster in surname order.

§

1 WILLIAM DING 丁磊

B. OCTOBER 1, 1971 (NINGBO, ZHEJIANG, CHINA)

William Ding is the founder and CEO of NetEase. He made significant contributions to the development of computer networks in mainland China. According to *Forbes'* China Rich List 2015, he is the 10th wealthiest person in China with an estimated fortune of 10.6 billion dollars.

H	D	M	Y
n/a	e己	f丁	m辛
n/a	d未	m酉 文昌學堂	r亥

BAZI SYSTEM • VARIABLE

	17	27	37	47	57
LUCK CYCLE	t乙	T甲	r癸	R壬	m辛
	d未	F午	f巳	W辰	t卯

The Self is moist Yin Earth. Born in a powerful Metal month of the Rooster, this Earth, being loosened by Metal crystals, is porous and feeble. With a Wood team of the Pig and Goat subjugating it further, the Self becomes a Follow type, laboring under the control of two conflicting flows: Wood and Metal. A wrong move could subject him to punishments from either one. This creates a tense life in which the Self must make sudden adjustments, striving for quick wins before the inevitable punishments set in.

Wood, being in a natural team, enjoys a slight winning edge. Not to be outdone, Metal derives strength from being in the prime of its cycle, spreading its signs strategically to keep the stronger Wood (Pig) in check. The war continues until a Yin Fire steps in to melt down the Metal, tipping the balance in favor of Wood. In fact, additional Fire turns out to be the vital ingredient of Ding's success.

In 1997, a Fire year when Yin Fire (f丁), entered his Goat period, he founded and became the CEO of NetEase. The Goat reinforced the power of his Wood team, while additional Fire disabled the Metal. In 2003, another Goat year taking place during his Horse period, he became the richest individual on the Chinese mainland. This time the Goat reinforced the Wood team, while the Horse Fire from his luck cycle succeeded in crippling Metal once again. In 2011, a Rabbit year occurring in the wake of this auspicious flow, we see NetEase's employees increasing to 6000 over a short span of 13 years.

One other special feature contributes to his success. The possession of a Yin Earth Goat day pillar (ed己未) qualifies him as one of the Intelligent Six. He is intellectually superior - a fast learner with enhanced decision-making capabilities. His intellectual capacity is further reinforced by the presence of a Scholar star (文昌) and a Study Hall star (學堂), both embodied in the Rooster of the month branch.

YEAR	AGE	LUCK CYCLE	KEY EVENTS
Prior to 1997	<26	Yin Wood, t乙	Graduated from Chengdu College of Electronic Science and Technology; worked as engineer
1997	26	Goat, d未	Found NetEase, introducing China's first dual language free email service to users
2003	32	Horse, F午	Richest individual in China
2004	33	Horse, F午	Won the Wharton Infosys Business Transformation Award

YEAR	AGE	LUCK CYCLE	KEY EVENTS
2012	41	Yin Water, r癸	NetEase had 7,098 employees, over 18% increase in a year
2015	44	Snake, f巳	The 10th wealthiest person in China with an estimated fortune of $10.6 billion

Andrew O'Keefe is an Australian entertainer and former lawyer, having begun his television career in 2003, a Goat (Wood) year, the same banner year as Ding.

Song Il-Gook is a Korean actor, who signed an exclusive contract with a new management company in 2015, during his Snake period.

Izabela Dragneva is a retired weightlifter from Bulgaria, representing her country in the Summer Olympics of 2000 and 2004 (the same banner year as Ding), and also winning gold medals in the European Championships of those years.

2 GUO GUANGCHANG 郭廣昌
B. FEBRUARY 16, 1967 (DONGYANG, ZHEJIANG, CHINA)

Guo Guangchang is the chairman of Fosun International Limited and a representative of the 12th Chinese People's Political Consultative Conference. In 2015, he was listed as the 34th richest person in China by *Forbes*, with a net worth of 7.3 billion dollars.

In 2007, Fosun International (00656.HK), the holding company of Fosun, was listed on the Hong Kong Stock Exchange. Fosun invested several billions in foreign firms, including Club Med of France, Portugal and Greece.

H	D	M	Y
n/a	m辛	R壬	f丁
n/a	r亥	T寅 陽貴	d未

BAZI SYSTEM • FOLLOW WEALTH

	14	24	34	44	54
LUCK CYCLE	M庚	e己	E戊	f丁	F丙
	R子	r亥	H戌	m酉	M申

The Self is Yin Metal, born in spring when Wood is thriving. With a Wood team of the Goat (d未) and the Pig (r亥) supported by Water, Wood becomes the dominant flow. The feeble Yin Metal Self submits to a Follow Wealth configuration.

The Yang Water (R壬) sitting in between the Pig and the Goat is well-poised to provide nourishment to the Wood team, indicating a strategic and goal-oriented individual. Clearly then, he benefits from Wood and Water, but dreads Metal.

Guo's Bazi benefits from certain special enhancements which may also have contributed to his quick and phenomenal success. Firstly, his Tiger is a powerful Nobleman (陽貴), well supported by Water. Secondly, as a Yin Metal Pig day pillar Self, he is likely to reap further good fortune in mid-life.[1]

In following the trajectory of his career, we see that he had a head start as a university teacher in 1989, immediately after graduating in his Rat (Water) period. In a Water year of 1992, he founded Guangxin, earning the initial capital for future investments.

His key accomplishment, the Fosun Group, began in 1995 at the age of 28. This happened to be a Pig year, taking place as Guo approached his own Pig period in the luck cycle. Fosun was soon to expand nationally and internationally. In 2007, another Pig year, Fosun International was listed on the Hong Kong Stock Exchange, while the Goat year of 2015 saw Guo earning his rightful place among the global elite of billionaires. It goes without saying that Wood and Water played a vital role in his success.

YEAR	AGE	LUCK CYCLE	KEY EVENTS
1989	22	Rat, R子	Graduated in philosophy from Fudan University; taught in the department
1992	25	Yin Earth, e己	Founded Guangxin Technology Development Company Ltd.
1993	26	Yin Earth, e己	Made a small fortune from the venture

---

1 The Pig (r亥) becomes the pairing partner of the Tiger (T寅) Nobleman (陽貴), this process rendering it an Assistant Nobleman of the Yin Metal Self. It is assigned to guide the Self to success. Since it is located in the third pillar, the Self is likely to reap its benefits during the third quarter of life.

YEAR	AGE	LUCK CYCLE	KEY EVENTS
1995	28	Pig, r亥	Founder and Chairman of Fosun Group; invested in insurance, pharmaceuticals, healthcare, property, mining, steel, retail, services and finance
1999	32	Pig, r亥	MBA from Fudan University
2007	40	Dog, H戌	Fosun International listed on HKSE (00656.HK)
2015	48	Yin Fire, f丁	The 34th richest person in China by *Forbes*, with net worth of $7.3 billion

Randall Brooks Phillips is a famous journalist from the United States. Public record of her life is sketchy; however, she certainly picked the right career given that a strong Wood flow supports the writing and printing fields. As ever, personal choice plays a key role in the vastly divergent fates of two individuals born on the same date. Although the energy potential is available to all, it takes motivated individuals to capitalize upon their beneficial flows.

3 LEI JUN 雷軍
B. DECEMBER 16, 1969 (XIANTAO, HUBEI, CHINA)

Lei is the founder of Xiaomi, a 45 billion-dollar technology company. In 2011, he was ranked at 201 on *Forbes'* annual list of China's 400 Richest. In 2014, *Forbes* named him "Businessman of the Year".

H	D	M	Y
n/a	t乙	F丙	e己
n/a	g丑	R子	m酉

BAZI SYSTEM · VARIABLE

	13	23	33	43	53
LUCK CYCLE	T甲	r癸	R壬	m辛	M庚
	H戌	m酉	M申	d未	F午

This Self has arguably the most fortunate system among all the samples in our current investigation as well as textbook cases in general. To begin with, the chart possesses an extremely rare "chain-breeding" feature. Moving clockwise from the day stem, this chain starts with the Wood Self breeding Fire, which in turn produces Earth. Such a short chain-breeding process alone would entitle a person to a lifetime of easy and bountiful wealth; in fact, its official term is literally translated as *Progressive Dining*. In this particular case, however, the Earth (e己) continues to extend the chain, giving birth to the Metal Rooster which, in its turn, yields the Rat - Water - that then comes full circle to empower the Wood Self. The extended chain guarantees the bearer of this chart an uninterrupted abundance of opportunities, as well as powerful, dependable energy. Such valuable features have naturally created a high achiever, one who may easily prosper by the structure of his pillars alone.

But it does not end there. As a Yin Wood Self born into a Rat Water month, with a potent team of Metal empowering this Water, Lei becomes Follow Resource. The Yang Fire flanking the Self in the month stem creates a glamorous plant, promoting his visibility on the world stage.

He prospers on Water and Metal, dreading Wood and dense Earth. From the table below, we can see how he scaled mountains during the Rooster and the Yang Water periods. In 2000, he founded online bookstore Joyo.com, when the Dragon of that year formed a Water team with his Rat. In 2004, when the Monkey of that year formed another Water team with his Rat, he sold the same company to Amazon for 75 million dollars.

As Lei's challenging elements, Wood and Earth were harmful to some degree but, overall, made little impact. During the Yang Wood Dog (TH甲戌) period of his luck cycle, Lei poured his efforts into preparations for a future career. Hard work and study are both effective means by which to offset any potential impact from harmful flows. In the Pig year of 2007, the Yang Wood hidden in the Pig threatened the security of his position. He resigned as CEO of Kingsoft, citing health concerns. Symbolically, the Yin Wood Self lost the fight to the stronger Yang Wood competitor and he was ousted, given that only one heir is entitled to stay. It seemed that he may intuitively have understood his destiny and moved with the flow to avoid any anticipated punishment, such as being fired from his high position.

Nevertheless, with such a blessed system, Lei was not to remain subdued for long. He swiftly rebounded to become the Chairman of UCWeb in 2008, founding his own company, Xiaomi, two years later.

YEAR	AGE	LUCK CYCLE	KEY EVENTS
1991	22	Dog, H戌	Graduated in computer science (Wuhan University); engineer for Kingsoft
1998	29	Rooster, m酉	President of Kingsoft
2000	31	Rooster, m酉	Founded Joyo.com, an online bookstore
2004	35	Yang Water, R壬	Sold Joyo.com for $75 million to Amazon.com
2007	38	Monkey, M申	Resigned as President and CEO of Kingsoft at year end for "health reasons"
2008	39	Monkey, M申	Became Chairman of UCWeb
2010	41	Monkey, M申	Founded Xiaomi, manufacturing smart phones, mobile apps, and other consumer electronics
2011	42	Monkey, M申	Rejoined Kingsoft as Executive Director
2012	43	Yang Water, R壬	"Top 10 Business Leaders of the Year" by China Central Television

YEAR	AGE	LUCK CYCLE	KEY EVENTS
2013	44	Yang Water, R壬	"The 11 Most Powerful Business people in Asia" by *Fortune*; award for "Most Notable Entrepreneur" by *BAZAAR* Men's Style
2014	45	Yang Water, R壬	Became the 8th richest person in China with a net worth of $9.9 billion; named "Businessman Of The Year" by *Forbes Asia*
2015	46	Yang Water, R壬	Xiaomi invested in more than 20 start-ups with plans for investing in 100 more

Craig White, born in Morley, England, is an English former first-class cricketer, and a relatively close counterpart of Lei Jun. In 2004, White was appointed Captain of Yorkshire, the same year that Lei Jun sold his company to Amazon for 75 million dollars. In 2012, White accepted a position on the coaching staff at Hampshire County Cricket Club, while Lei Jun was ranked among the top 10 business leaders in China. They both resigned once during a challenging time: White from his captaincy at the end of 2006, a potent Fire/Earth year, and Lei in early 2007, a Fire/Wood year.

DJ D-Wrek, born in California, United States, is a touring DJ working in hip-hop and pop music.

Michelle Smith (née Michelle Smith de Bruin), from Ireland, was a triple Olympic gold medalist at the Atlanta Games. She was tainted by controversy over drug use in the Rat year of 1996 at the age of 27, though the claims were unsubstantiated. The Rat, her Nobleman, exerted its protective influence and despite a subsequent four-year ban from swimming 1998, she was never stripped of the 1996 gold medals. Interestingly, the ban effectively ended Smith's sporting career, and she went on to become a barrister-at-law. A great Bazi system does bring swift and easy success. However, it takes personal initiative to navigate through adversity and reinvent oneself in the process.

4 LI YANHONG (ROBIN) 李彦宏
B. NOVEMBER 17, 1968 (YANGQUAN, SHANXI, CHINA)

Robin Li co-founded the Chinese search engine Baidu. In September 2015, he was ranked the seventh richest man in mainland China with a net worth of 9.6 billion dollars.

H	D	M	Y
n/a	m辛	r癸	E戊
n/a	t卯	r亥	M申

BAZI SYSTEM · FOLLOW WEALTH

	16	26	36	46	56
LUCK CYCLE	t乙	F丙	f丁	E戊	e己
	g丑	T寅	t卯	W辰	f巳

The Self is Yin Metal, unsupported by the cold month into which he was born. Sitting atop a Wood team of the Pig and the Rabbit (his money element), he is greatly enfeebled. The Wood team, empowered by rain on the stem and irrigation from the Water contained within the Monkey, is supremely powerful, capable of transforming the chart to a system of Follow Wealth. Water and Wood become his leading flow; he dreads additional Metal as it hurts the Wood flow and disrupts his Follow configuration.

As a Follow Wealth type (Wood), he is financially savvy, attaining riches quickly and easily. The Follow status produces an intelligent individual that is adaptable and goal-oriented, while the chart's abundant Water bestows grace and refinement upon the Metal Self.

Although it does not directly contribute to his wealth, Fire achieves three helpful things: it curtails the force of Metal, adds shine and glamour to the tree leaves, and also warms up his cold Water, making for a comfortable life.

Li's most dramatic breakthrough took place in 2000, when he successfully co-founded Baidu. This was a Dragon year taking place in his Tiger phase, when the Dragon joined the Tiger and his day-pillar Rabbit to form the most powerful Wood trio, bountifully rewarding him in the process. His greatest moment of glory came in 2015 when he took the spot as seventh richest man in China, and the 119th richest man in the world. Another Wood trio was at work this time around, formed when the Goat of that year joined the Pig and the Rabbit in his Bazi.

The Metal impact was obvious. He studied hard during his Metal Ox period, and failed to fulfill plans to earn a Ph.D. Fortunately, he completed a masters degree and was soon on track to success. The chart below details the many major milestones that were achieved in Fire years and luck cycles.

YEAR	AGE	LUCK CYCLE	KEY EVENTS
Prior to 1991	<23	Ox, 己丑	BSc in information management from Beijing University
1991-1994	23-26	Ox, 己丑	MSc in Computer Science from University at Buffalo
1994-1997	26-29	Yang Fire, 丙	Joined IDD Information Services, a division of Dow Jones; developed software program for online edition of *The Wall Street Journal*

YEAR	AGE	LUCK CYCLE	KEY EVENTS
1996	28	Yang Fire, F丙	Awarded a US patent on search engine service
1997-1999	29-31	Yang Fire, F丙	Engineer for Infoseek, a pioneering search engine
2000	32	Tiger, T寅	Co-found Baidu, the largest Chinese search engine, with over 80% market share by search query
2005	37	Yin Fire, f丁	Baidu successfully completed its IPO on NASDAQ
2007	39	Yin Fire, f丁	Baidu became the first Chinese firm in the NASDAQ-100; Li appeared in *CNN Money*'s annual list of "50 People Who Matter Now"
2011	43	Rabbit, t卯	One of the "15 Asian Scientists To Watch" by *Asian Scientist Magazine*
2014	46	Yang Earth, E戊	Appointed by UN Secretary General as co-chair of the Independent Expert Advisory Group on Data Revolution for Sustainable Development

YEAR	AGE	LUCK CYCLE	KEY EVENTS
2015	47	Yang Earth, 戊	Ranked as the 7th richest man in China, the 119th richest man in the world, according to the Hurun Report Global Rich List 2014

Sean Edward Miller is a distinguished American college basketball coach. He was born to an athletic family, with a father and brother who were also basketball coaches. Family background played a key role in his career choice. The focused and powerful Wood team, on the other hand, set him apart as a leader in his field.

5 LI ZHONGCHU 黎中蹰
B. FEBRUARY 1, 1964 (CHINA)

Zhongchu Li is the chairman and founder of Beijing Shiji Information Technology, providing IT support to hotels in China. In May 2015, his net worth was reported to be in the regions of 4 billion dollars.

H	D	M	Y
n/a	{M庚 天德 月德	t乙}	r癸
n/a	W辰	g丑 陽貴	t卯

BAZI SYSTEM · VARIABLE

LUCK CYCLE	18	28	38	48	58
	r癸	R壬	m辛	M庚	e己
	r亥	H戌	m酉	M申	d未

The Self is Yang Metal. Empowered by a Dragon (strong Earth) and an Ox (Earth, Metal), he is a strong Metal Self, fully capable of managing and controlling his financial resources. Yin Wood, his financial element and the money sign to Yang Metal, comes in a pair empowered by rain and is equally strong. In fact, the configuration of a Yin Wood standing directly next to the Yang Metal Self is known as *Money Seeking the Self* - the Self is consistently and effortlessly rewarded. As discussed in Chapter Three, stems M庚 and t乙 form a natural pair. From the table below, we can see why he prospered so phenomenally in 2005 and 2015, both Yin Wood years. As the financial resources of his Metal Self, Yin Wood was figuratively swarming into his pocket. The Yin Wood Rooster year of 2005 is even more auspicious: while Yin Wood brought him money, the Rooster made him Dominant Metal, increasing his capacity to hold and control the incoming financial gains. That year he became the chairman of his firm.

Furthermore, the system can easily form a Dominant Self configuration with the onset of a Rooster or Snake from his luck cycle or external cosmic flows. The firm grew quickly during his early 40s as a Dominant Metal in his Rooster period, when it rode on the Chinese tourism boom during which hotel chains sought more efficient service.

Since Earth is so bountiful in the chart, the onset of additional Earth could also create a Follow Resource configuration. This occurred in 1998 (ET戊寅), a Yang Earth year, right at the beginning of his Dog (Fire and Earth) period at the age of 34. He set up a firm which grew exponentially over the next few years, becoming fully established during his Rooster period, and providing software to more than 6000 hotels.

YEAR	AGE	LUCK CYCLE	KEY EVENTS
c. 1985	21	Yin Water, r癸	Graduated from Wuhan University in space physics
1987	23	Pig, r亥	Master's degree in engineering, doing IT repair work in China Ministry of Aerospace
1998	34	Dog, H戌	Quit job to set up Beijing Shiji IT, operating from his bedroom
2005	41	Yin Metal, m辛	Chairman of his firm since January 2005
2015	51	Yang Metal, M庚	Net worth reported to be $4 billion

Linus Roache is an English actor from Manchester, United Kingdom. Some of his most notable years took place from 2000 to 2002 in his Dog period, aged 34 to 36, during which he starred in several film and television productions, and was nominated or won awards including Best Actor. These later accomplishments appear to have been set in motion by the earlier acclaim he received in the Dog year of 1994, where he took the lead role in the film *Priest* (1994), bringing his talents to the attention of a wider audience. Arguably, he has succeeded as a Follow Resource type.

Bugge Wesseltoft is a Norwegian jazz musician, pianist, composer and producer, son of the jazz guitarist Erik Wesseltoft. Bugge Wesseltoft had a great impact on the Norwegian Jazz scene during the 1990s.

Sharon Bruneau is a Canadian model and retired professional female bodybuilder. She retired from competitive bodybuilding after the Yang Wood Dog year of 1994.

6 LIU QIANGDONG (RICHARD) 劉強東
B. FEBRUARY 14, 1974 (SUQIAN, JIANGSU, CHINA)

Richard Liu is the co-founder of JD.com or Jingdong Mall, one of the leading e-commerce industry leaders in China. With JD.com's IPO in the United States on May 22, 2014, his net worth surged to 6.1 billion dollars.

In his early years, Liu maintained an active interest in politics, intrigued by its connection to China's political elite. In 1996, he graduated with a bachelor's degree in sociology from the People's University of China, immediately after which all his spare time was invested into teaching himself computer programming in a bid to catch up with economic trends. Liu later earned an EMBA from the China Europe International Business School.

H	D	M	Y
n/a	F丙 月德	F丙 月德	T甲
n/a	H戌	T寅 學堂	T寅 學堂

BAZI SYSTEM · VARIABLE

LUCK CYCLE	16	26	36	46	56
	E戊	e己	M庚	m辛	R壬
	W辰	f巳	F午	d未	M申

As a Yang Fire Self with a Fire alliance of the Tiger and the Dog, Liu enjoys Dominant Fire status, with a strong and plentiful supply of Wood feeding it constantly. The individual is healthy, confident, motivated, goal-oriented, visionary and consistently high-achieving. To enjoy the full potential of Dominant Fire, however, a Horse is required to form the full Fire trio. In 2014, Liu was at the cusp of his own Horse luck cycle at the age of 40, and on May 22 of that year, he took JD.com public on the NASDAQ. After the IPO, Liu's worth surged to around 9.4 billion dollars, making him one of the 100 richest men in China.

H	D	M	Y
n/a	r癸	e己	丁甲
n/a	f巳	f巳	F午

MAY 22, 2014

As ever, there are additional features further contributing to the good fortune of this Bazi. Firstly, the day pillar (FH丙戌) alone places him in the elite class of individuals discussed in Vladimir Putin's system in Chapter Five. The Self is guided to succeed by an invisible hand.

Secondly, as a Yang Fire Self with one or more Tigers in his Bazi, he could readily prosper with the onset of a Dragon from the cosmos or from his own Dragon luck cycle. Such is the superiority of this con-figuration that the Dragon is precluded from clashing with the Dog in his Bazi, given that the latter is tightly bound up with the other Tiger sign. We see the positive effects of the Dragon period when Liu landed a job in 1996, which conferred the skills and credentials he needed to then go on to start his own business a couple of years later.

Thirdly, two *Yue De* stars serve as protection from lurking evils and danger. In fact, the possession of two of these stars is a sure sign of becoming wealthy. Finally, the presence of two Study Hall stars bestows great intelligence on the bearer, ensuring a lifetime of oppor-tunity to acquire and apply knowledge. This would explain how Liu succeeded in gaining computer-programming proficiency through self-study alone.

The beneficial elements for his system are Fire, Wood, Metal and Earth - Fire provides the energy which the Self requires to conquer; Wood sustains this Fire, while Metal rewards him with financial gain; Earth protects by forming a barrier against Water. As it hampers Fire, Water becomes the dreaded enemy of his chart.

YEAR	AGE	LUCK CYCLE	KEY EVENTS
1996	22	Dragon, W辰	Director of a Japanese health product enterprise
1998	24	Dragon, W辰	Started own business, Jingdong, as distributor of magneto-optical products
2003	29	Yin Earth, e己	Opened 12 stores in the chain
2004	30	Yin Earth, e己	Launched his first online retail website; later that year founded JD.com
2005	31	Yang Metal, M庚	Closed all physical stores, diverting them online
May 22, 2014	40	Horse, F午	JD.com went public on the NASDAQ; stock price rose about 15%. After the IPO, Liu was worth around $9.4 billion, making him one of the 100 richest in China

We did not find any visibly successful individuals born on the same day in China. Worlds apart in Europe, however, two are found to be harnessing the power of Fire's mastery over Metal.

Valentina Vezzali is an Italian fencer. She has mastered the sword to win six Olympic gold medals in foil competitions, and many other gold medals in the World Fencing Championships and European championships between 1995 to 2013. With a plethora of stunning achievements under her belt, she then became a member of the Italian Chamber of Deputies as part of the Scelta Civica party in 2013.

Matt Redman is an English Christian worship leader in the United Kingdom who later became a singer-songwriter and author, music and the voice being in the Metal domain.

7 MA HUATENG 馬化騰
B. OCTOBER 29, 1971 (SHANTOU CITY, GUANGDONG, CHINA)

H	D	M	Y
n/a	f丁	E戊	m辛
n/a	r亥 陽貴 (壬甲)	H戌 (戊辛丁)	r亥 陽貴 (壬甲)

BAZI SYSTEM • VARIABLE

	16	26	36	46	56	66
LUCK CYCLE	F丙	t乙	T甲	r癸	R壬	m辛
	M申	d未	F午	f巳	W辰	t卯

Ma Huateng, also known as Pony Ma, is the founder, president and CEO of Tencent Inc., one of the largest internet companies in China. The company controls China's biggest mobile instant messaging service, its subsidiaries providing media, entertainment, internet and mobile phone value-added services. Ma is a deputy to the fifth Shenzhen Municipal People's Congress and serves in the twelfth National People's Congress.

The Self, as Yin Fire born in late fall, is weak. The two Wood elements (his Pig signs) are blocked by a great wall of Yang Earth and the Dog (EH戊戌) from being able to support the Self. To prosper, he needs a team consisting of a Goat, a Rabbit, or both, to pull the Pigs together and form a supreme Wood team. This would then allow him become Follow Resource.

The other option is to be Dominant Fire, having either a Tiger or a Horse form a Fire team with the Dog in the month pillar, and inviting the two Pigs to lend their support. Somehow in the course of Ma's life, all these potentialities materialized. In the Rabbit year of 1999 when Ma was 28, he co-launched a software, OICQ, which quickly garnered more than a million registered users by the year's close. During his Goat period, aged 31 to 35, his company, Tencent, became the largest Chinese instant messaging service with a 74 per cent share of the market. Its IPO in June 2004 on the Hong Kong Stock Exchange raised 200 million dollars, quickly making him one of the world's most influential people at the age of 36 (*TIME*, 2007). At 44, during his Horse period, the Goat of 2015 conferred Dominant Fire status and he became one of *Forbes'* top 50 richest people in the world.

It is worth noting that the auspicious features contributing to his stellar success are exceptionally rare. To begin with, as in Lei Jun's case discussed earlier, Ma also possesses the *Progressive Dining* configuration, bestowing a lifetime of easy and uninterrupted abundance.

Secondly, there is a mutual exchange of Money stars between the day and the month pillars - that is, Yin Fire's Money star (m辛) is hidden in the Dog, while Yang Earth's Money star (R壬) is hidden in the Pig. This criss-crossing structure indicates money coming to the Self from a variety of sources.

Thirdly, the Self has two Noblemen (his Guides). With one directly below, and both representing his Resource element, they guide him in making judicious decisions. The Resource element also enhances good reputation. Yang Earth - his Yang offspring (傷官) - is a powerful ally flanking him from the month stem, ensuring visibility and a swift path to fame.

YEAR	AGE	LUCK CYCLE	KEY EVENTS
1993	22	Monkey, M申	Graduated in Computer Science from Shenzhen University, working with China Motion Telecom, developing software for pagers
1998	27	Yin Wood, t乙	Co-found Tencent with four classmates
1999	28	Yin Wood, t乙	Co-launched software, OICQ, quickly garnering over a million registered users by the end of 1999
2000	29	Yin Wood, t乙	Changed OICQ into QQ after losing a lawsuit
2003	32	Goat, d未	Tencent released its own portal (QQ.com) and made forays into the online games market (Goat year)
2004	33	Goat, d未	Tencent became the largest Chinese instant messaging service; raised $200 million in June's IPO on HKSE
2005 (tm乙酉)	34	Goat, d未	Tencent launched the C2C platform Paipai.com, competing with Alibaba
2007 (fr丁亥)	36	Yang Wood, T甲	One of the world's most influential people (*TIME*)
2015 (td乙未)	44	Horse, F午	One of the top 50 richest people in the world

Matthew Hayden is a former Australian cricketer. He was a powerful and aggressive left-handed opening batsman, holding the record for the highest score made by an Australian batsman in Tests (380). He retired from all forms of cricket in September 2012 aged 41, just one year following the end of all the Wood flows in his luck cycle.

Cricket is a game played on a grass field, an area of substantial Wood flow. Did this environment contribute to Hayden's success? The idea would be impossible to substantiate either way, though interestingly, Tiger Woods (who bears cosmically-supportive first and last names) has Wood as his useful element and also plays on grass. Some may contest this, arguing that Ma succeeded exponentially without the same environmental support. Nonetheless, it must be conceded that Ma has always resided near a coastal city, rich in the flow of Wood and Water.

Lee Stephen Mason is an English professional football referee. Since 2006 (Horse period), Mason has been on the list of the Select Group Referees who officiate in the Premier League.

8 JACK MA 馬雲
B. SEPTEMBER 10, 1964 (HANGZHOU, ZHEJIANG, CHINA)

Jack Ma is the executive chairman and founder of Alibaba Group, as well as the first mainland Chinese entrepreneur to have appeared on the cover of *Forbes*. He is tenacious, entrepreneurial, and relentlessly innovative, having had the courage to connect China to the internet in 1995 upon the discovery that it had no presence on the worldwide web at the time. With wealth statuses changing constantly over time, he still remains one of the few top-ranking billionaires in China.

H	D	M	Y
n/a	R壬	r癸	T甲
n/a	H戌	m酉	W辰

BAZI SYSTEM · VARIABLE

	19	29	39	49	59
LUCK CYCLE	t乙	F丙	f丁	E戊	e己
	r亥	R子	g丑	T寅	t卯

The Self is Yang Water - a river - born in a Rooster month when the Metal flow is at its most powerful, capable of producing crystal clear water. The clear Water symbolizes either good looks or a good mind and in fortunate cases, both. He is strong, energetic, ambitious, and above all, intelligent. His critical defect? There is another Water vying for support, rendering the system one of Sibling Rivalry. The bearer must deal with many challenges on the path to success.

To prosper, Ma has to solve the rivalry issue by becoming a Dominant Water Self. This takes place whenever a Rat or Dragon shows up externally or from the luck cycle, and first occurred for Ma in the Rat year of 1996, when his China Yellow Pages generated huge revenue. In 1999 to 2000 during his own Rat period (aged 34 to 38), he won 25 million dollars in foreign venture capital investment.

Another way to prosper is by having a Snake or Ox join his Rooster, forming a Metal team to empower the Self. This took place from ages 44 to 48, when Ma received numerous awards and accolades recognizing excellence in the field of business.

A third way of circumventing Sibling Rivalry can be achieved by using Yang Earth to pair up the Yin Water (r癸), his Sibling competitor - such an event would then confer Follow Resource status. This took place from 2013 to 2017 during his Yang Earth (E戊) period between the ages of 49 to 53, when once again, over 25 billion dollars was raised at Alibaba's initial public offering on the New York Stock Exchange. It went on to become one of the most valuable tech companies in the world, as well as having the largest IPO in US financial history. Ma served as the executive chairman of Alibaba Group, later becoming a top-ranking global billionaire.

Do not overlook the magic of the Yin Fire which represents *Money Seeking the Self.* It took place from 2003 to 2007 between ages 39 to 43 during his Yin Fire period. At this juncture, Ma founded Taobao and various other revenue-generating sites, attracting an investment of 1 billion dollars from Yahoo. The honors and awards received during this period eventually also brought further financial gain.

In summary, though Ma possesses a faulty system, his fortunate luck cycles have more than remedied its flaws, bestowing a sequence of great fortune in the prime window of his life.

YEAR	AGE	LUCK CYCLE	KEY EVENTS
1988	24	Yang Fire, F丙	BA in English, Hangzhou Normal University; lecturer in English & International Trade at Hangzhou Dianzi University
1995-1997	31-33	Yang Fire, F丙	Started China Yellow Pages after visiting US, dedicated to creating company websites. Within 3 years, it had made 5 million Chinese yuan ($800,000)
1999-2000	35-36	Rat, R子	Alibaba twice won a total of a $25 million in international venture capital investment, to create an e-commerce platform for Chinese enterprises to address World Trade Organization (WTO) issues
2003	39	Yin Fire, f丁	Founded Taobao, Alipay, Ali Mama and Lynx, garnering support from Jerry Yang with a $1 billion investment
2005 (tm乙酉)	41	Yin Fire, f丁	"Young Global Leader" by the World Economic Forum; one of the "25 Most Powerful Business people in Asia" by *Fortune* magazine
2006	42	Yin Fire, f丁	eBay shut down its own site in China, avoiding competition

YEAR	AGE	LUCK CYCLE	KEY EVENTS
2007	43	Yin Fire, f丁	Selected by *Business Week* as "Business person of the Year"
2008	44	Ox, g丑	One of the 30 "World's Best CEOs" by *Barron's*
2009	45	Ox, g丑	One of the world's 100 most influential people (*TIME*)
2010	46	Ox, g丑	One of "Asia's Heroes of Philanthropy" for his contribution to disaster relief and poverty, by *Forbes Asia*
2012	48	Ox, g丑	Invited to lecture at Wharton School of Finance, MIT, Harvard University, and Beijing University
2013	49	Yang Earth, E戊	Awarded an honorary doctoral degree by the Hong Kong University of Science and Technology in November
2014	50	Yang Earth, E戊	Alibaba raised over $25 billion in IPO on the NYSE, one of the most valuable tech companies in the world; largest IPO in US financial history; Ma served as executive chairman of Alibaba Group
2015td	51	Yang Earth, E戊	Honored with the "Entrepreneur of the Year" award at The Asian Awards

Donna De Lory is an American singer and songwriter. She was born in Calabasas, California, to well-known musician parents, the act of following in the footsteps of one's parents being a characteristic feature of those enjoying Follow Resource status. She capitalized on her Metal flow.

Both she and Ma were born with great talent. At the outset, De Lory was nurtured by a supportive environment in a wealthy country with musical parents to kick-start her career. On the other hand, Ma had to strike out on his own in a severely competitive environment, with limited resources for the struggling entrepreneur. As an English major, and later an English lecturer, not known to be particularly proficient in mathematics, Ma surmounted major obstacles to master the fast-paced and technical domain of the internet. He thrived on challenges and diversified his talents to access the great opportunities that China offered in his time. It bears emphasizing once again that habitat and personal choice makes a crucial difference to our destiny.

One wonders quite naturally why such a great system did not produce more individuals in China succeeding on a similar momentum. Taking into consideration the severe lack of resources and opportunity in Ma's time, it would still be close to impossible to find someone possessing his sheer iron will to succeed!

9 WANG CHUANFU 王傳福
B. FEBRUARY 15, 1966 (WUWEI, ANHUI, CHINA)

H	D	M	Y
F丙 月德	t乙	M庚	F丙 月德
H戌 華蓋	f巳	T寅	F午

BAZI SYSTEM • VARIABLE

	16	26	36	46	56
LUCK CYCLE	R壬	r癸	T甲	t乙	F丙
	W辰	f巳	F午	d未	M申

Chuanfu Wang is a trained chemist and founder of the BYD Company. Being born to peasant farmer parents and orphaned in high school, he was raised by his siblings. He has a bachelor's degree in chemistry and a master's degree from the Beijing Non-Ferrous Research Institute.

Wang's Shanghai-based company, BYD, is the world's largest manufacturer of mobile phone batteries; it also manufactures electric cars. The company has grown from 20 employees in 1995 to over 170,000 in recent years. Both he and BYD have received thousands of patents and numerous awards around the world.

Two versions of his birthday exist on the internet: April 8, 1966 and February 15, 1966. The latter has been widely and consistently used in Chinese internet circles. Exceptionally, a birth hour is also available, with his full four-pillars chart being openly discussed in forums without raising any objections from Wang.

In checking the birth pillars with his life events, the February 15 birthday makes much more sense as compared to April 8, which hardly bears relevance. The following discussion utilizes therefore the February 15 date. As an exception, and in the absence of any open objection from Wang since its publication on the internet, we have also included the birth time to facilitate our explorations.

The Self is a plant. With two Yang Fire fame elements shining upon his leaves and bestowing glamour, he is confident, dignified, and destined to stand tall above the herd. His Power element, the Yang Metal (M庚) stands shoulder to shoulder with his Yin Wood Self, trimming and refining the plant. This individual is highly cultivated, disciplined, and possesses great integrity.

A powerful Fire team of the Horse, Tiger and Dog is reinforced by two more Fire elements in the stems. They all work together to enfeeble the plant, creating a perfect Follow Children system and setting the bearer on a smooth path to monumental success. The Snake, however, stands in the midst of the Fire team, blocking the Dog from joining its two teammates - a possible indication of marital or health-related issues.

In another scenario, as each branch contains hidden Earth, the onset of additional Earth could confer a Follow Wealth status. Wang is fortunate in having the benefit of two complementary Follow types, all in the same family. His helpful elements are Fire and Earth, while Water and Wood are the most harmful. As the manufacture of batteries nurtures his Fire and Earth flows, Wang seems to have chosen his career intuitively, with both his system and career mutually assisting and empowering each other.

During the Dragon period, with the additional Earth protecting his Fire, he happily completed his education, taking a research position shortly after. Next, Yin Water set in, along with restlessness and dissatisfaction. Wang sought a change and tentatively began the process of setting up his own company. Once he entered the Snake period, with its mixture of Fire and Earth - additional Fire and Earth also arriving opportunely from the year flow of 1997 - we see an exponential growth in the company, most evidently in the number of its employees, which increased from 20 in 1995 to a sizeable body of 15,000 by 2000, a span of little more than five years.

At the onset of the Yang Wood period, Wang found himself under the challenge of his dreaded foe, and his ambitions for the firm grew more elaborate. He initiated the painstaking process of listing BYD on the Hong Kong Stock Exchange. This kept him on his toes for the next few years, although not much else is known about the Yang Wood impact during this time. Typically, a Wood Self with Follow status is likely to experience significant setbacks on encountering another Wood Sibling. In Wang's case, however, the potent strength of Fire leaves little room for the onset of additional Wood to cause much of an impact. The competence and resourcefulness of the Self helps too of course.

With the advent of dynamic Fire from the Horse during his early forties, Wang became the richest man in China. By the time he reached the Yin Wood phase which followed, however, it was reported that his sale of electric cars was struggling. Yet by the close of 2015, BYD had become the best-selling electric vehicle manufacturer in the world. As a Yin Wood Goat year (td乙未), the Goat joined his Snake (f巳) and Horse (F午) to form a Directional Trio of Fire, powerfully outweighing the Yin Wood effect from his luck cycle at this juncture. The Self succeeded on the support of an empowering boss. After a mixed year of 2016, his luck surged again in 2017, a Fire and Metal year. The external annual flow always plays a key role in our luck cycle.

YEAR	AGE	LUCK CYCLE	KEY EVENTS
1990	24	Dragon, W辰	Master's degree from the Beijing Non-Ferrous Research Institute; worked as a government researcher
1995	29	Yin Water, r癸	Co-founded BYD, manufacturing batteries for mobile devices, energy storage and electric cars
1997	31	Snake, f巳	Business grew by 100% for three consecutive years
2002	36	Yang Wood, T甲	Employees grew to 15,000; BYD was listed on HKSE
2008	42	Horse, F午	Warren Buffett bought 225 million new shares of BYD
2009	43	Horse, F午	Worth $5.1 billion, he became China's richest man (*Hurun Report*)
2015	49	Yin Wood, t乙	BYD became world's best-selling electric car manufacturer

Kim Myers is an American television and film actress. Her breakthrough role was in the 1985 horror classic, *A Nightmare on Elm Street 2* (1985), possibly attributable to the Earth contained in the Ox of that year. We have, however, no other significant events to reflect the impact of the flows.

10 ZHANG XIN 張欣
B. AUGUST 24, 1965 (BEIJING, CHINA)

Zhang comes from a long line of Chinese immigrant merchants who settled in Burma. In the wake of anti-Chinese sentiment across Southeast Asia in the 1950s, her parents moved back to China, their ancestral homeland, where Zhang was eventually born.

Together with her husband Pan Shiyi, Zhang co-founded SOHO China, the largest commercial real estate developer in Beijing. They further founded the SOHO China Foundation in 2005 as a philanthropic organization, engaging in education initiatives to alleviate poverty. In July 2014, the SOHO China Foundation announced that the SOHO China Scholarships would be a 100 million-dollar initiative, endowing financial aid scholarships at leading international universities. The foundation signed a 15 million-dollar gift agreement with Harvard University in July 2014, and a 10 million-dollar gift agreement with Yale University in October 2014. As of 2014, Zhang is listed as the 62nd most powerful woman in the world by *Forbes*, known for being one of China's most celebrated female entrepreneurs.

H	D	M	Y
n/a	M庚	T甲	t乙
n/a	H戌 (戊辛丁)	M申 (庚壬戊)	f巳 (戊丙庚)

BAZI SYSTEM • VARIABLE

	15	25	35	45	55
LUCK CYCLE	F丙	f丁	E戊	e己	M庚
	H戌	r亥	R子	g丑	T寅

The Self is Yang Metal. Born in a prime Metal and Water month, she is blessed with either intelligence or beauty. The Yang Metal is also supported by three other Metal elements and nurtured by two strong Earths. This is a strong Metal Self, able to take command of her financial resources, these being the two Wood elements in the stems. The number of Metal signs in the chart indicate that the system could potentially fall into a Sibling Rivalry configuration. However, since all the other Metal signs are grounded or hidden within the branches, unable to compete, the Self will emerge victorious in any Sibling conflict. From her energy system alone, it is apparent that she needs to work hard for a living, tirelessly warding off the continuous threats to her well-being. Nevertheless, her pillars provide ample opportunity to prosper upon the onset of beneficial flows.

Firstly, she could quite easily become a Dominant Metal with the onset of a Rooster joining her Monkey and Dog to form the most powerful Metal trio. Alternatively, a Rooster or Ox could also join the Snake to form a Metal alliance, depending on the circumstances. We see this scenario taking place in the Rooster year of 1993 when, fresh from graduation and as a foreigner with very limited work experience, she secured a position at Goldman Sachs in New York.

In the Ox year of 2009, Zhang was among those listed in *Forbes'* "Top Ten Billionaire Women We Admire" as well as the *Financial Times'* "Top 50 Women in World Business". At age 50 in the Rooster year of 2015, Zhang entered her own Ox period, garnering awards, honorary titles and wide recognition, her net worth soaring to an excess of 3 billion dollars. In 2017 during the same Ox period, she entered *Forbes'* China Rich List at number 69.

On the other hand, the Self could achieve Follow Resource status with the onset of additional Earth or Fire, a development which did in fact bring Zhang the greatest fortune. In her Yin Fire period from the ages of 25 to 29, Yin Fire empowered the Earth already abundant in her chart. She earned a master's degree from Cambridge, and secured positions with two leading firms in the United States, two monumental accomplishments for a woman who had started out as a poverty-stricken factory laborer. Armed with the invaluable training she had received abroad, Zhang returned to Beijing, married a successful property developer at 30, and co-founded SOHO China. From the age of 35, Zhang became a household name and a powerhouse in the world of real estate development, her company logo emblazoned on the sides of buildings all over Beijing. With the property development reinforcing her Earth flow, she became a true Follow Resource.

The remarkable versatility of her system means that Zhang is also capable of adopting Follow Children status should her month branch Monkey encounter either a Rat or Dragon, assimilating itself into a powerful Water team to bestow ready success and fame. This took place in her Rat period from the ages of 40 to 44.

YEAR	AGE	LUCK CYCLE	KEY EVENTS
1992-1993	27-28	Yin Fire, f丁	Received MA in Development Economics from Cambridge University; worked for Goldman Sachs
1994	29	Yin Fire, f丁	Worked for Travelers Group
1995	30	Yin Fire, f丁	Returned to Beijing, China; married, co-founded Soho China, a property firm with husband Pan Shiyi
2004	39	Yang Earth, E戊	Won *BusinessWeek*'s Stars of Asia Award
2007	42	Rat, R子	Selected as one of the "Ten Women to Watch in Asia" by the *Wall Street Journal*

YEAR	AGE	LUCK CYCLE	KEY EVENTS
2009	44	Rat, R子	Included among *Forbes'* "Top Ten Billionaire Women We Admire"
2010	45	Yin Earth, e乙	Named among "China's Top 10 Career Women Role Models of 2009" by the All-China Women's Federation
2011	46	Yin Earth, e乙	Listed in "The International Power 50" and the "Most Powerful Women" by *Fortune*; again recognized as one of "World's Most Powerful Women" (*Forbes*)
2014	49	Yin Earth, e乙	Listed as the 62nd most powerful woman in the world by *Forbes*

Marlee Beth Matlin is an American actress, author, and high-profile member of the National Association of the Deaf. Having lost her sense of hearing from the age of 18 months, she did not allow the disability to hinder an otherwise distinguished acting career. Matlin seemed to enjoy the flows of Fire and Earth, sharing banner years with Zhang in various pursuits. She won the Best Actress Academy Award at the age of 21 for her part in *Children of a Lesser God* (1986), the only deaf performer ever to have done so. Other awards came in 1987 at age 22, and in 2004 at age 39, all won during periods of Yang Earth, which transformed her into a Follow Resource Self.

Like Zhang, Matlin has demonstrated courage and tenacity in the face of adversity, and is a champion of several humanitarian causes. She has been a source of inspiration to those with disabilities, particularly among deaf and hearing-impaired communities, saying, "The greatest handicap of deafness does not lie in the ear; it lies in the mind."

Reggie Miller is an American former professional basketball player. After 18 seasons with the Indiana Pacers, he is widely considered the Pacers' greatest player of all time as well as the highest-paid Pacer in franchise history. Currently, he works as an NBA commentator for TNT. On September 7, 2012, Miller was inducted into the Naismith Memorial Basketball Hall of Fame.

§

At the completion of the chapter, let us sum up our key findings in Figure 7a, below.[2]

What has been the role of cosmic energy in the making of a billionaire in China? To begin with, the impact of the current leading, (or dominant) cosmic flow of the eighth Feng Shui period clearly determines the group winners - the intelligent, young males mentioned at the beginning of this chapter. But why have only a handful of such males excelled above all others, and who are they?

Straight away, we can see that all of our billionaires set up their companies at an early age, ranging from 24 to 37, with more than half below the threshold of age 30. They each possess a superior category of Bazi system, nine belonging in the Variable category, and two in the Follow Wealth. Of the Variable charts, at least one of the possible configurations are Follow at some point or other. Most of the charts have no less than one special star, while some possess a range of good stars with various energy-enhancing functions.

---

2 This summary includes the case study of Wang Jianlin, already discussed in Chapter Four (p.47).

ENERGY SYSTEM	Variable 9			Follow 2	
ENVIRONMENT	Coastal or waterfront cities 7	Inland cities 3		Mixed 1	
AGE AT FIRM'S INCEPTION	24-30 6			31-37 5	
USEFUL ELEMENTS	Metal 3	Wood 4	Water 6	Fire 5	Earth 5
EDUCATION	Engineering / Science 6				
	Economics 2				
	Sociology 1				
	English 1				
	Philosophy 1				

Fig. 7a: Summary of Chinese Billionaires

The Variable Selves truly live up to their cosmic definition, yielding and adapting to opportunities as and when they arise. We may comfortably conclude that phenomenal achievements have their roots in a higher grade of cosmic energy system, so fundamental as it is to success. As the different system types imply, we require discipline (to follow and obey the leading flow) and an open mind (variability) to reap rewards. These qualities are particularly imperative in a competitive environment hindered by limited resources, such as China.

But what gave this select group the edge over a myriad others born on the same day? There are many variables. Success comes from the interaction of Yin and Yang forces. In terms of habitat, these billionaires were all born, worked, or educated in one of the most prolific cities or provinces on the east coast of China. Six have their businesses headquartered in Beijing, two in Shenzhen, and two in Shanghai and Hangzhou, all top line cities. They are benefiting, therefore, from the returning flows of interacting with the most productive and stimulating energy available to them.

The physical environment of these cities, with the exception of some shortfall in Metal flow, also reflects the balance of the five elements, supporting a variety of cosmic systems. Interestingly, this Metal deficit is also apparent in the distribution of useful elements among the samples - only three of the 11 case studies require Metal as one of their useful elements. Typically, those such as Wang Chuanfu, Wang Jianlin and Zhang Xin rely heavily on Fire and Earth as useful elements, adopting Fire or Earth-related businesses in their careers. The two Wangs were also raised in an Earth-rich province.

Education plays a key role, despite the persistence of college-drop-out success stories; after all, the lack of a formal qualification does not suggest never having been educated at all. There are those who simply assimilate knowledge at a faster rate, graduating ahead of schedule or striking out alone before completing formal education. The Chinese billionaires in this sample all hold one degree or more, predominantly in technology and science. The few who missed out on an IT-related education either picked up the necessary skills on their own or went into real estate.

Personal choice makes a difference. Globally, many people born at the same time possess a similar potential but few are able to catch the right wave. Modern China is almost completely IT-centric. Eight of the billionaires are in IT-related businesses, meeting the evolving needs of a modern population. These Follow types are able to yield to the demand and flow with the tide.

CHAPTER EIGHT

MODERN RUSSIAN BILLIONAIRES

Throughout its long history and vast territory, Russia has never been short of billionaires. We have taken a sample from among the top 20 richest Russians compiled by *Forbes* (2015) for the following reasons. Firstly, they are a group of modern self-made billionaires, offering distinctive insights into how the classical system of Bazi works in the present age. Secondly, their elaborate biographies are easily accessible, fully furnished with the birth data needed to satisfy the criteria for our study. Thirdly, of the 20 notable figures, 16 have at least one counterpart with a duplicate Bazi. Among the 16, one has already been used as an illustration in Chapter Four, leaving the remaining 15 to be discussed here in surname order.

§

1 ROMAN ABRAMOVICH
B. OCTOBER 24, 1966 (SARATOV, RUSSIA)

Roman Abramovich is a businessman, politician, and the primary owner of private investment company, Millhouse LLC. He set up and liquidated at least 20 companies during the early 1990s, the majority of these falling into the retail sector, but also comprising businesses as varied as retreading car tires and bodyguard recruitment. According to *Forbes*, Abramovich's net worth in 2015 was 7.8 billion dollars, making him the 12th richest person in Russia, and the 137th richest person in the world.

H	D	M	Y
n/a	F丙 月德	E戊	F丙 月德
n/a	W辰	H戌	F午

BAZI SYSTEM • VARIABLE

	15	25	35	45	55
LUCK CYCLE	M庚	m辛	R壬	r癸	T甲
	R子	g丑	T寅	t卯	W辰

The Self, as Yang Fire supported by a Fire team of the Dog and Horse, belongs to a Dominant Fire configuration - strong enough to control the Metal and command riches. On the other hand, born in a powerful Earth month on an earthy day and surrounded by four other Earth elements, he may tend to follow the lead of Earth, possessing a Follow Children system instead. In this scenario, Metal would become his most beneficial element.

As a college student in his Yang Metal period, Abramovich began his career selling commodities. He soon amassed a major fortune between the ages of 25 to 34 during the powerful Metal period of his Yin Metal Ox (mg辛丑), by which time he had elected to work within the Metal-related field of oil and plastics, intuitively following the tide of this beneficial flow. Indeed, from his case history we can see that he has prospered chiefly during the Metal flows of his luck cycle, which span a period of almost 20 years from the age of 15, creating a chain of children (his Wealth element) giving birth to children. The feature denotes an extending or expanding fortune.

The Bazi is also blessed by certain additional features conferring similar good fortune. First, being a Yang Fire sitting on a Dragon (W 辰), he could easily obtain wealth or fame by encountering a Tiger (T 寅), creating the special link WT辰寅.[1] From his key events below, we can see that he did in fact make a name for himself as an effective and caring governor of Chukotka during his Tiger phase from ages 40 to 44; his assets also grew exponentially over the same period.

Second, Abramovich possesses two *Yue De* (月德) stars in the stems, these being the two Yang Fire elements (丙). A Bazi code expounds that "two *Yue De* leads to money falling from the sky." Third, as Fire is so prevalent in the chart, the onset of a Rabbit could transform his Bazi into a state of Fire Transformation.[2] That happened in his Rabbit period which began after 2015, at the age of 49.

---

1 Chapter Three contains a more detailed discussion on these Bazi features, p.32.
2 Also known as a Merging state, this system was discussed in *Four PIllars of Destiny, Discover Your Code to Success*, p.140

YEAR	AGE	LUCK CYCLE	KEY EVENTS
Prior to 1988	<22	Yang Metal, M庚	Attended Gubkin Institute of Oil and Gas in Moscow; sold retreaded car tires and commodities, making a small fortune
1989-1991	23-25	Yin Metal, m辛	Chairman of the Comfort Co-op (plastic toys) in 1989, director of the ABK small enterprise in Moscow, 1991
1992-1995	26-29	Yin Metal, m辛	Founded 5 companies in producing, retailing and trading oil and oil products
1995	29	Yin Metal to Ox, m-g辛-丑	Acquired half of Sibneft, a large oil company, with an associate of Boris Yeltsin, each partner paying $100 million, which rapidly became billions
1996	30	Ox, g丑	Established another 10 firms
1999-2008	33-42	Yang Water to Tiger, R-T壬-寅	Governor of Chukotka; greatly upgraded the region with $1.3 billion of his own money
2015	49	Rabbit, t卯	The 12th richest person in Russia, and the 137th richest person in the world

His birthday is also owned by three notable individuals across three continents, all in fields of high visibility.

Zahn McClarnon is a Native American Lakota-Irish actor from Colorado. He shared a banner year with Abramovich in 1990, during their Metal period, when he moved to Los Angeles to pursue a career in acting. This turned out to be a fortunate move, as Zahn's varied and successful career shows.

Jing Haipeng is the first Chinese astronaut to fly on two space missions. He joined China's Shenzhou space program in the powerful Earth year of 1998 at the age of 32, prospering as Abramovich did during the same Ox period.

Matthew Warchus is a British director and dramatist.

2 VAGIT ALEKPEROV
B. SEPTEMBER 1, 1950 (BAKU, AZERBAIJAN)

Vagit Alekperov, an Azerbaijani and Russian businessman, became President of leading Russian oil company, LUKOIL, in 1993. He was born in Baku, a center of the international petroleum industry, and began his work in its oil fields at the age of 18.

In 2014, he was rated by *Forbes* magazine as the eighth richest person in Russia with a net worth of 12.3 billion dollars, and the 114th richest person in the world.

H	D	M	Y
n/a	e己	T甲	M庚
n/a	r亥 (甲壬)	M申 (戊庚壬)	T寅

BAZI SYSTEM · VARIABLE

	12	22	32	42	52
LUCK CYCLE	F丙	f丁	E戊	e己	M庚
	H戌	r亥	R子	g丑	T寅

The Self is moist Earth - enfeebled by three Woods and two Metals, the Earth becomes a Follow type. Alas, he is caught between two combative bosses, Wood and Metal. He follows one at a time, so as not to anger the other; his choices are circumstantial. As a consequence, the configuration has led to the creation of a tense personality, one that is hard-working, vigilant and quick to seize upon opportunities.

Which is the stronger boss? By the number of signs, Wood is slightly ahead; yet in terms of timing, Metal is much the stronger, being in its prime season of September. Metal is also strategically poised to best control the Wood. Thus, without the additional onset of Wood, he follows Metal, adopting a Follow Children system. The Wood elements, after all, perform a role to keep the Earth enfeebled.

On the other hand, additional Wood in the form of a Goat or Rabbit could easily create a Wood team, transforming the leading flow to that of Follow Power. Alekperov advanced from an engineer to a production manager during his Pig period, while a Rabbit year saw him promoted to General Director of the production company Kogalym Neftegaz.

In practice, however, many of his notable achievements took place during the Rat period, when the Rat and the Monkey in his Bazi formed an alliance of Water. It seems that the two Water elements (R 壬) in his Bazi (contained within the Pig and Monkey), being themselves empowered by two Metal elements, also had a chance to create a leading flow, forming a Follow Wealth system.

The many possibilities expounded here point to a marked versatility of character. Overall, Metal seems to be his dominant flow, with the majority of momentous achievements taking place during Metal years. Earth is the most detrimental element, as it breaks up his Follow status. He suffered hardships throughout most of his Yang Earth period. In 1979, a Yin Earth year, an explosion on his rig threw him into the stormy Caspian Sea, where he had to swim for survival.

YEAR	AGE	LUCK CYCLE	KEY EVENTS
1974	24	Yin Fire, f丁	Graduated from the Azerbaijan Oil and Chemistry Institute; worked as a drilling operator in a Caspian regional oil production firm

YEAR	AGE	LUCK CYCLE	KEY EVENTS
1979-1984	29-34	Pig, r亥	Advanced from engineer to deputy head of production unit, working in extreme conditions on oil platforms
1985	35	Yang Earth, E戊	First deputy general director of Bashneft production company, a Metal year
1987	37	Rat, R子	General director of production company, Kogalymneftegaz
1990	40	Rat, R子	Appointed deputy minister of the Oil and Gas Industry of the Soviet Union, the youngest deputy energy minister in Soviet history
1991	41	Rat, R子	Created the first integrated state-owned energy company, Langepas-Uray-Kogalymneft, later becoming LUKoil Oil Company
1993	43	Yin Earth, e己	President of LUKoil, one of the world's most powerful oil companies, with reserves second only to Exxon

YEAR	AGE	LUCK CYCLE	KEY EVENTS
2000	50	Ox, g丑	LUKoil acquired Getty Petroleum Marketing and its 1,300 gas stations in the US, the first American acquisition by a Russian company
2006	56	Yang Metal, M庚	Moved into banking and media, being one of the two main owners of IFD Kapital Group
2014	64	Yin Metal, m辛	Rated by *Forbes* as the eighth richest person in Russia with a net worth of $12.3 billion and the 114th richest person in the world

Between two celebrities born on the same date, the case history of **Phil McGraw** comes closest to that of Alekperov in terms of financial status and education. He is an American television personality, author, psychologist, and the host of television show *Dr. Phil*, which debuted in 2002 - a versatile talent. The year 1979 was monumental for both. While Alekperov suffered a near-death experience in the Caspian Sea, McGraw had just earned his Ph.D. in clinical psychology, leaving university to strike out on his own in an unknown field.

The year 1990 was another momentous step forward for the two individuals. Alekperov was appointed deputy minister of the Oil and Gas Industry of the Soviet Union, a move which led him into an elite circle of billionaires. Meanwhile, McGraw joined lawyer Gary Dobbs to co-found Courtroom Sciences, Inc. (CSI), a trial-consulting firm. The firm was later hired by Oprah Winfrey in a move which cemented their friendship and enabled McGraw to gain celebrity status as a guest on her talk show. Eventually, CSI became a profitable enterprise, advising Fortune 500 companies and achieving settlements for injured plaintiffs.

In 2014, Alekperov was rated by *Forbes* magazine as the eighth richest person in Russia with a net worth of 12.3 billion dollars. Meanwhile, *Forbes* listed McGraw's earnings at 70 million dollars for the 12 months of 2014, and ranked him the 15th highest-earning celebrity in the world. Both individuals display an aptitude for diversification and versatility within their chosen fields of expertise - Alekperov in business and commerce; McGraw in hosting talks, consultancy, and producing several best sellers over the course of his varied career.

Phillip Fulmer from Tennessee, United States, is a dedicated sportsman. He started playing football in 1968 at the age of 18, coaching in 1972 and head coaching from 1992 to 2008. Thereafter, he became a sports analyst on CBS's SEC Postgame Show, as well as various programming on the CBS College Sports Network. Fulmer was inducted into the College Football Hall of Fame in 2012, a year he enjoyed as Dominant Water.

3 PETR OLEGOVICH AVEN
B. MARCH 16, 1955 (MOSCOW, RUSSIA)

Petr Aven, the son of a professor of computer science, is an international businessman, economist and politician. Besides heading Alfa Bank, Russia's largest commercial bank, he is also a member of the board of directors at Letter One Group, established in 2013 to invest in international projects related to energy, telecommunications and technology. His papers on economic and trade issues have been highly valued and quoted in the financial and trade press on matters of Russian economy.

H	D	M	Y
n/a	F丙	e己	t乙
n/a	R子	t卯	d未

BAZI SYSTEM • FOLLOW RESOURCE

	13	23	33	43	53
LUCK CYCLE	f丁	F丙	t乙	T甲	r癸
	g丑	R子	r亥	H戌	m酉

The Self is Yang Fire; born on a rainy day, he is very feeble. Fortunately, he was born in mid-spring when Wood thrives. Further supported by a Wood team in the branches, he follows the leading flow of his Resource element, a favorable system indeed. His beneficial elements are Wood and Water. With the onset of a Pig, the existing partial alliance would be elevated into a full Wood team, conferring yet greater favor and fortune.

What happened during the Pig period of his luck cycle? It began in 1993 when Aven turned 38, and continued for five years. During this time, he became a political candidate in 1993, and a president and shareholder of Alfa Bank Russia in 1994, events which paved the way for future successes. Additional signs of a Goat or Rabbit would also reinforce his partial Wood team to great effect. This happened in the Goat year of 2015, when he was listed at number 301 in *Forbes'* annual World's Richest, with a net worth of some 5.1 billion dollars.

His dreaded elements are Metal and Fire. During the Yang Fire period, he studied hard to build a career. We have no discussions on how he fared in Metal years.

YEAR	AGE	LUCK CYCLE	KEY EVENTS
1977-1980	22-25	Yang Fire, F丙	Graduated from Moscow State University with Ph.D in Economics, 1980
1989-1991	34-36	Yin Wood, t乙	Senior researcher at the USSR Academy of Sciences and International Institute for Applied Systems Analysis in Luxembourg and Austria
1991-1993	36-38	Pig, r亥	Minister of Foreign Economic Relations for the Russian Federation, on high-level economic missions to Western capitals

YEAR	AGE	LUCK CYCLE	KEY EVENTS
1994-2011	39-56	Pig to Yang Wood to Dog to Yin Water, r-T-H-r 亥-甲-戌-癸	Shareholder and President of Alfa-Bank Russia
2013	58	Rooster, m 酉	Joined the board of Letter One Group, investing in telecoms, technology and energy sectors across 32 countries
2015	60	Rooster, m 酉	301st richest person in the world, with a net worth of around $5.1 billion

Bob Ley, also born on this day, is a sports anchor and reporter for ESPN in the United States. A multiple Emmy Award winner, he is the longest tenured on-air employee of the network.

4 OLEG DERIPASKA
B. JANUARY 2, 1968 (DZERZHINSK, RUSSIA)

Oleg Deripaska, raised in Ust-Labinsk, is Chairman of the Basic Element supervisory board, as well as President of En+ Group and United Company RUSAL, the largest aluminum company in the world. In 2015, he was listed among the 20 wealthiest people in Russia. His wealth has been estimated at 5.2 billion dollars by *Forbes* as of May 2017.

In 2001, he forged a powerful political alliance when he married the daughter of Boris Yeltsin's ex-chief of staff, Valentin Yumashev. The Yeltsin clan eventually connected him on friendly terms with Vladimir Putin.

H	D	M	Y
n/a	m辛	R壬	f丁
n/a	d未 華蓋	R子 文昌 學堂	d未

BAZI SYSTEM · VARIABLE

LUCK CYCLE	18	28	38	48	58
	M庚	e己	E戊	f丁	F丙
	H戌	m酉	M申	d未	F午

This is a shaky changeable system, creating an agile, aggressive and resourceful individual. The Metal Self, born in a cold town near Moscow, needs warm Earth in order to thrive. Being supported by two Earth elements (the two Goats in his chart), he becomes a Follow Resource, following the lead of Earth. This Earth, however, frozen and containing substantial Wood, is far from a good provider to a Follow type. To prosper, he needs hot Earth.

Nevertheless, a fortunate feature can be found in his month pillar. The Rat, as his Scholar and Study Hall combined in a single sign, anchors his life embankment, creating an excellent student who succeeds in applying his knowledge to new ventures.

As a physicist, Deripaska graduated at the wrong time - 1989, in the midst of the breakdown of the Berlin Wall. Although unable to secure a job at the that juncture, he was able to apply the laws of physics to successfully navigate his life path over uncharted turbulent waters. During the Yang Metal phase of his luck cycle, the stronger Sibling transitioned him into a Sibling Rivalry system. With lack of money as an ever-present threat, he realized that in order to sustain himself he would need to shift his focus from theoretical physics to basic survival. As a consequence, he undertook casual work on construction sites, this move having the inadvertent bonus of injecting a greater flow of Earth into his system, thus bolstering his ability to tide over an otherwise challenging period.

As he moved into the Dog period (H戌), he collaborated with various physics and engineering associates to start the Metal trading company VTK, which, besides generating income, connected him to some influential people. He also began to use the profits derived from the company to purchase shares in the Sayanogorsk Aluminum Smelter in Southern Siberia, eventually going on to secure a 20 per cent stake in the plant, reaping the benefits of the Follow Resource configuration.

At the age of 26 in 1994, the Dog year arrived with its hot, strong Earth. Riding on the crest of his Earth flow, Deripaska became the director general of the factory. Over the next five years of his moist Earth period (e 乙), he became the main shareholder of the smelter, as well as the president of the Sibirsky Aluminum Investment Industrial Group, later the core asset of RUSAL, which went on to become one of the largest aluminum producers in the world under his leadership.

In 2001 at the age of 33, Deripaska entered the Rooster period, immediately becoming Dominant Metal when the Snake from that year joined the Rooster from his luck cycle to form a Metal alliance. With this development, his fortunes surged: by marriage, he was connected to the Yeltsin clan and, eventually, to Vladimir Putin, resulting in a solid and long-term relationship. His good Earth extended for the next five years, and in little under a decade, he became a member of the global billionaires club.

How can we assess the compatibility and quality of the relationship between Vladimir Putin and Deripaska? As discussed in Chapter Five, Putin's Yang Fire Self joins with Deripaska's Yin Metal Self to form a natural compatible pair. Putin's rich Earth flow also serves to enrich Deripaska's system. When going through a good luck cycle, we naturally encounter the right mentors to help us.

YEAR	AGE	LUCK CYCLE	KEY EVENTS
1993	25-28	Dog, H戌	Teamed up with fellow scientists to set up a Metal trading company, VTK, applying a scientific approach to commodity trading
1994	26	Dog, H戌	Bought required shares in the Siberian smelter to become its general manager
1996	28	Yin Earth, e己	Economics degree from the Academy of Economics
2000	32	Yin Earth, e己	Took over the Siberian aluminum factory, eventually controlling the aluminum industry in Russia

YEAR	AGE	LUCK CYCLE	KEY EVENTS
2001	33	Rooster, m酉	Connected to the top political elite in Moscow (Yeltsin clan/Vladimir Putin) by marriage
2004-2007	36-39	Rooster to Yang Earth, m-E酉-戊	Represented Russia in the Asia-Pacific Economic Co-operation Business Advisory Council, chairing the Russian National Committee of the International Chamber of Commerce
2008	40	Yang Earth, E戊	Wealth estimated by *Forbes* at $28 billion, the ninth richest man in the world
2017	49	Yin Fire, f丁	Fortune declined to around $5 billion, rebounding from the huge drop from his Monkey (Yang Metal) period

Four notable individuals share this birthday with Deripaska.

Cuba Gooding Jr. is an American actor born in New York, United States. Both he and Deripaska share certain features, not least a coincidental likeness in their humorous facial expressions and smiles. Both are talented individuals - where Deripaska struggled to make ends meet before eventually striking gold, the more privileged Gooding was able to glide smoothly in the footsteps of his parents to become an entertainer in his own right.

Like Deripaska, he also saw through a challenging period of taking on odd jobs before achieving fame between 1992 to 1994, his Dog period. In the Snake Earth year of 2001 when Gooding was 33, he was able to capitalize on a fruitful surge in creativity with the release of four feature films. This was the same year that connected Deripaska to the political elite in Moscow.

Anky van Grunsven is a Dutch dressage champion who holds the record for the most Olympic medals won by any equestrian athlete, and is the only rider to record three successive Olympic wins in the same event. She has won numerous medals at the World Equestrian Games. Interestingly, she won her first medal (silver) at 24, the transition phase of her Rabbit period which conferred Follow Wealth status. At age 32 in the Earth year of 2000 (MW庚辰), she won her first gold medal in the Olympics. Her success and medal wins continued into the next 15 years of Fire and Earth.

Chris Spencer, born in California, is a Jamaican American actor, comedian and producer.

Martin G. Xuereb was a commander of the armed forces of Malta.

5 SERGEY GALITSKY
B. AUGUST 14, 1967 (LAZAREVSKY, SOCHI, RUSSIA)

Sergey Galitsky is a Russian businessman, founder and co-owner of Magnit (Russia's largest retailer), headquartered in Krasnodar, southern Russia. Krasnodar is the commercial center of Southern Russia and has the highest number of malls in Russia, as well as the lowest unemployment rate among the cities of the Southern Federal District. In June 2014, *Forbes* listed him as the 13th wealthiest Russian, with a net worth of 11.2 billion dollars.

H	D	M	Y
n/a	M庚 ↘	↙E戊	f丁
n/a	H戊 華蓋 （丁戊辛）	M申 （戊庚壬）	d未 陰貴 （丁己乙）

BAZI SYSTEM · VARIABLE

LUCK CYCLE	12	22	32	42	52
	F丙	t乙	T甲	r癸	R壬
	F午	f巳	W辰	t卯	T寅

The Self, as a Yang Metal born in a prime Monkey month, possesses either great intelligence or physical charms. Earth, in a team of three empowered by Fire, becomes the leading flow. The system falls into two possible categories. As long as the Monkey stays intact, it will be governed by Sibling Rivalry, with the Self fighting to overcome a myriad obstacles. Yet if the Monkey were to be neutralized in some way, the system could qualify as Follow Resource, prospering swiftly and monumentally. This scenario may take place when either of two conditions are met: firstly, if the onset of a Rat or Dragon transforms the Monkey into Water, and secondly, if the onset of a Snake anchors the Monkey, precluding it from taking action.

One other feature enhances his success. A *Sibling-crossing* between the month and day pillars (indicated by arrows in the chart above) means that the Yang Metal day stem (M庚) has its Sibling hidden in the month branch, while the Yang Earth month stem (E戊) has its Sibling in the day branch. This configuration brings a substantial degree of friendly or brotherly support to all of his endeavors whenever such assistance may be called upon. It leads to the creation of a good leader, and in this case, a popular merchant. Clearly, this feature has been well utilized in the building of Galitsky's retail conglomerate. He also benefits from the guidance of a Nobleman (陰貴) to keep him on the right path, and a Talent star (華蓋) in the spousal palace, bestowing personal talent as well as the collaboration of a gifted spouse.

From his case history, we can observe that Galitsky's good fortune did indeed begin with the onset of a Snake at the age of 27. The Snake disabled the Monkey, swiftly creating a Follow Resource configuration. He founded three profitable retail establishments one after the other. The opening years of the Snake period were all powerful Earth years. The Yang Wood Dog in 1994 and the Yang Earth Tiger of 1998 served to empower the flow in his luck cycle. The Dragon, another strong Earth year which disintegrated the Monkey into Water, cleared a way for the Follow Resource system, putting Magnit on the road to exponential growth. Additional Earth followed in 2009, a powerful year of the Yin Earth Ox (eg己丑), and again in 2014, year of the Yang Wood Horse (TF甲午), potent Fire reinforcing his Earth flow and earning Galitsky a place in the club of global billionaires.

YEAR	AGE	LUCK CYCLE	KEY EVENTS
1985-1987	18-20	Horse, F午	Served in the Soviet army

YEAR	AGE	LUCK CYCLE	KEY EVENTS
1989	22	Yin Wood, t乙	Worked in a bank; took a loan, selling perfume and cosmetics
1993	26	Yin Wood, t乙	Graduated from the Economics Faculty of Kuban State University
1994	27	Snake, f巳	Founded TransAsia, distributing cosmetics and fragrances. Closed the shop; founded Tander, to develop food discounters
1998	31	Snake, f巳	Opened first grocery store, Magnit
2006	39	Dragon, W辰	Magnit conducted its IPO, valued at $1.9 billion, growing annually at an average of $2 billion
2009-2010	42-43	Yin Water, r癸	Ranked 35th of Russia's richest people (*Forbes*)
2014	47	Rabbit, t卯	Listed by *Forbes* as the 13th wealthiest Russian, with a net worth of $11.2 billion

William Prunier, a French soccer player, has had a vastly different career, enjoying a smooth life path as both player and coach, mostly in France. After all, the *Sibling-crossing* did grant him plenty of supportive fans as well as distinction in his chosen field.

6 GERMAN KHAN
B. OCTOBER 24, 1961 (KIEV, UKRAINE)

German Khan is a Russian businessman of Ukrainian-Jewish descent. His business interests are concentrated within the oil and gas industries. Khan studied at the Moscow Institute of Steel and Alloys, specializing in steel production. In 2015, he became one of Russia's top 20 billionaires.

H	D	M	Y
n/a	M庚	E戊	m辛
n/a	T寅	H戌	g丑 陽貴

BAZI SYSTEM · VARIABLE

LUCK CYCLE	15	25	35	45	55
	F丙	t乙	T甲	r癸	R壬
	M申	d未	F午	f巳	W辰

This is a rare marvel of a system, with Khan being the sole individual from amongst his same-day birth counterparts to have been able to capitalize on its unique features.

Firstly, the Self, as Yang Metal, with a strong Yin Metal in the year pillar, falls officially into a Sibling Rivalry configuration. As the stronger Metal Self, however, he is able to elbow his Sibling from contention to become the victor. Secondly, with an Ox in the year branch, the onset of a Snake or a Rooster, would make him Dominant Metal, a great achiever. Lastly, with the onset of a Horse, he becomes Follow Power, enjoying easy, phenomenal success and its accompanying high position. As a Variable type, Khan is unusually blessed.

From his case history, we can see that he was able to seize upon the dominant flow each time it occurred. In the Snake year of 1989, he co-founded Alfa Group Consortium and became its chairman. In his own Snake period from the ages of 50 to 54, he was emboldened to venture into international expansion, teaming up with Mikhail Fridman to establish the LetterOne Group, which operated out of 32 countries. It became the base from which he was able to amass the substantial fortune that eventually landed him in the top 20 of Russian billionaires, aged 55 (2015, td乙未).

In 1990 (MF庚午) at the age of 29, Khan became a full Follow Power on the formation of a Fire trio, selling his company, Alfa Group Consortium, for a profit. In 2003, Khan found himself in the Horse period of his luck cycle, aged 42, becoming once again a full Follow Power, and the executive director of TNK-BP.

YEAR	AGE	LUCK CYCLE	KEY EVENTS
Prior to 1988	<27	Monkey, M申	Studied steel industry at the Moscow Institute of Steel and Alloys
1988	27	Yin Wood, t乙	Worked in a wholesale business selling clothes, footwear and jewelry
1989	28	Yin Wood, t乙	Co-founder and Deputy Chairman of Alfa Group Consortium with Alexander Furmon, making clothes
1990	29	Yin Wood, t乙	Sold company for a profit
1992-1998	31-37	Goat to Yang Wood, d-T未-甲	Held various managerial posts in Alfa Group

YEAR	AGE	LUCK CYCLE	KEY EVENTS
2003	42	Horse, F午	Executive director of TNK-BP, in charge of oil business development, a joint venture with BP
2013	53	Snake, f巳	Left the company; joined Mikhail Fridman in establishing Letter One Group, based in Luxembourg, operating in 32 countries

Gary Thomas is an American Evangelical minister, a writer of Christian literature, and best-selling author of 19 books. He shared a special year with Khan in 2003, when *Authentic Faith* (2002) won, amongst others, the Gold Medallion Award in the Christian Living category.

Chris Carmichael, from Miami, Florida, is a retired professional cyclist and endurance sports coach as well as the founder of Carmichael Training Systems. Athletes under his tutelage have reportedly won a combined total of 33 medals at the Olympics, World Championships, and Pan American Games.

Mary Bono is a former US Representative for California's 45th congressional district, serving from 1998 to 2013.

7 ALEXEY KUZMICHEV
B. OCTOBER 15, 1962 (KIRON, RUSSIA)

Alexey Kuzmichev is one of the co-founders and controlling own-
ers of Alfa Group. He also indirectly controls a substantial percentage
of VimpelCom Ltd. (now VEON), the world's sixth largest mobile
network operator; Alfa Bank, Russia's largest private commercial
bank; and X5 Retail Group, Russia's largest food retailer.

Forbes magazine listed Kuzmichev at 138 amongst the world's
richest people in 2013, with a fortune estimated at 8.8 billion dollars.

H	D	M	Y
n/a	F丙 ↘	↙M庚	R壬
n/a	H戌 華蓋 (丁戊辛)	H戌 華蓋 (丁戊辛)	T寅 學堂

BAZI SYSTEM · VARIABLE

	18	28	38	48	58
LUCK CYCLE	R壬	r癸	T甲	t乙	F丙
	R子	g丑	T寅	t卯	W辰

The Self is Yang Fire. With a Fire alliance of the Dog (H戌) and
Tiger (T寅), he is, by definition, Dominant Fire. In reality, however, this configuration barely functions as his habitat is too cold, and
would require the support of strong Wood or additional Fire in order
to function optimally. On the other hand, with two Dogs providing
rich and abundant Earth, he has a better chance of prospering from a
Follow Children (Earth) system. Above all, he dreads Water, thriving
instead on Wood or Earth.

A host of other helpful factors bolster Kuzmichev's luck. As seen in Galitsky's chart above, there is a *Sibling-crossing* feature between the day and month pillars; that is, the stems on the day and month pillars have their Siblings found in each other's branches. The configuration creates a bountiful and ready source of intimate support. With a Study Hall star (學堂) in the year branch, the Self is a fast learner, capable of applying new knowledge to profitable endeavors. Meanwhile, the two Talent stars (華蓋) promote deep thinking, artistry, and management skills, those possessing this star often preferring solitude over the company of others.

During his Water periods from ages 18 to 33, he worked hard at a series of menial jobs, struggling to build meaningful career connections. The little success he enjoyed in 1988 came from the good Earth flow of that Dragon year, during which he founded Alfa Photo. At the age of 36 in 1998, another Earth year occurring towards the last leg of his Ox Earth period, he founded Alfa Eco, the luck turning once again.

Kuzmichev is responsible for overseeing Alfa Group's international trading operations. He continued to prosper during Wood periods which boosted his Fire flow. As soon as he entered the Rabbit Wood period, he ranked among the world's billionaires. We can see that a Fire Transformation[3] took place with the pairing of the Dog and the Rabbit. With both the Fire team and the Fire merging working in tandem, a true Dominant Fire was created.

---

3 See *Four Pillars of Destiny, Discover your code to Success* p.140

YEAR	AGE	LUCK CYCLE	KEY EVENTS
1980-1982	18-20	Yang Water, R壬	Served in the army on the Russian-Chinese border as radio operator
1983	21	Yang Water, R壬	Enrolled in the Moscow Institute of Steel and Alloys, meeting future business partners, Fridman and Khan
1988	26	Rat, R子	Founded Alfa Photo
1998	36	Ox, g丑	Founded Alfa Eco
Since 1998	36	Into 20 years of Wood	Oversaw Alfa Group's international trading operations, working in Europe, Venezuela, Nigeria, Iran and Iraq
2013	51	Yin Wood to Rabbit, t-t乙-卯	The 138th richest person in the world with a fortune estimated at $8.8 billion

Nick Holt, from California, United States, is a football coach, enjoying a successful career as both player and coach.

8 VLADIMIR LISIN
B. MAY 7, 1956 (IVANOVO, RUSSIA)

Vladimir Lisin is a Russian steel tycoon and the chairman of Novolipetsk, one of Russia's four largest steel companies. He has a doctoral degree in metal engineering from the Moscow Institute of Steel and Alloys, and another in economics. As one of the world's leading authorities on metallurgical processes, Lisin holds various patents in the field, and has published over 100 articles on metallurgy and economics.

H	D	M	Y
n/a	T 甲	r 癸	F 丙
n/a	H 戊	f 巳	M 申
	(丁戊辛)	(庚丙戊)	(戊庚壬)

BAZI SYSTEM · VARIABLE

	10	20	30	40	50	60
LUCK CYCLE	T 甲	t 乙	F 丙	f 丁	E 戊	e 己
	F 午	d 未	M 申	m 酉	H 戊	r 亥

The Self is a feeble tree following two flows. Earth seems slightly ahead, being in a team of two and empowered by Yang Fire in the year stem with a further two Fire elements hidden in the branches. Water, also in a group of two, is empowered by some Metal to function as a total Water team. To varying degrees, the Self functions under both Follow Resource and Follow Wealth systems.

Yet the system is not without its challenges. As Earth and Water are conflicting in nature, Lisin requires additional help to prosper. This could take the form of more Earth to help impede the flow of

Water, or alternatively, more Metal or Water to lead the way. The bottom line is that he prospers chiefly on Earth and Metal/Water, but only one at a time. His most dreaded element is Wood. Fire works both ways: it controls the Wood and strengthens the Earth, but could also hurt the Metal. These conflicting scenarios create an adaptable individual, quick to forge ahead and seize opportunities.

Prior to the age of 24, Lisin fell into a Wood Sibling case during his predominantly Wood periods. At 19, he was working in a coal mine. By 24, during a Goat period of mixed flows, he made slight progress, attending college and going on to become a welder foreman after graduation.

In 1986, aged 30, with the joint effort of great Fire from the year and the Yang Fire period to boost his Earth flow, he became a deputy chief engineer of the company.

In 2013, a Snake year of Fire and Earth taking place during his Dog period at the age of 57, Lisin was rated the second richest man in Russia with a net worth estimated at 24 billion dollars. These distinctive events demonstrate the function of Earth in creating a Follow Wealth system.

However, Metal and Water seem to be his best allies. He had chosen, perhaps intuitively, to work with metal since studying metallurgy in college. This course of study evidently enriched the Metal flow in his system. Its good work showed up in the Yang Water Monkey year of 1992 (RM壬申) when Lisin was 36, a Water/Metal year taking place during his Monkey (Metal and Water) period; he joined a group of traders who won control of Russia's steel and aluminum industry. When the partners split in 2000 (MW庚辰), a Metal year, he gained 13 per cent of the firm and later managed to secure a controlling share.

At 45 he entered his own Metal (Rooster) period, whereby the Metal and Water worked together to create a Follow Resource system. During the next few years of Rooster, he became the chairman and director of JSC Novolipetsk Iron & Steel Corporation, as well as

serving as director of various other entities, his assets growing exponentially all the while.

YEAR	AGE	LUCK CYCLE	KEY EVENTS
1975	19	Horse, F午	Mechanic in Soviet coalmine
1979	23	Yin Wood, t乙	Graduated from the Siberian Metallurgic Institute
1980-1986	24-30	Yin Wood to Goat, t-d乙-未	Welder foreman at Tulach-ermet Metals Works, rising to section manager, shop manager in 1979 (ed己未) and deputy chief engineer in 1986 (FT丙寅)
1989	33	Yang Fire, F丙	Professor at the Academy of National Economy
1992	36	Monkey, M申	Joined a group of traders (the Trans-World Group) who won control of Russia's steel and aluminum industry
1993-1998	37-42	Monkey to Yin Fire, M-f申-丁	Board member of several leading Russian Metal pro-ducers, a member of the board of directors of Novolipetsk Steel (NLMK) since 1996, and its chairman since 1998
2000	44	Yin Metal, m辛	Won a controlling share of Trans-World Group

YEAR	AGE	LUCK CYCLE	KEY EVENTS
2002-2009	46-53	Yin Metal to Yang Earth, m-E辛-戊	Chairman and Director of JSC Novolipetsk Iron & Steel Corporation; Director of OJSC United Shipbuilding Corporation
2013	57	Dog, H戌	The second richest man in Russia

Anne Dudley (England) and **S. Scott Bullock** (California, United States) are both musicians who prospered from Metal flows.

9 ANDREY MELNICHENKO
B. MARCH 8 1972 (GOMEL, BELARUS)

Melnichenko is a Russian businessman and billionaire. With an estimated personal wealth of 8 billion dollars, he ranked 137th in the *Forbes'* World's Billionaires list in 2015 (12th in Russia), aged 43. He is a major shareholder of EuroChem, SUEK, and SGC, as well as the chairman of the Strategy Committees of all three entities.

H	D	M	Y
n/a	{E戊	r癸}	R壬
n/a	{H戊 Power	t卯} Power	R子

BAZI SYSTEM · VARIABLE

	19	29	39	49	59
LUCK CYCLE	t乙	F丙	f丁	E戊	e己
	f巳	F午	d未	M申	m酉

This is a remarkably fortunate system. To begin with, there is a *Heaven and Earth Pairing* - stem pairings and branch pairings between the month and day pillars, Er戊癸 and Ht戊卯, indicated by brackets in his Bazi. Such a configuration confers top positions on the individual, often bestowing expertise in an exclusive field. It usually belongs to inventors succeeding in a unique endeavor.

Secondly, there is an exchange of Power elements between the two stems of Yang Earth (E戊) and Yin Water (r癸): here, the Rabbit (t卯) in the month branch is the Power element of the Yang Earth (E戊) day stem, while the Dog (H戊) in the day branch is the Power element of the Yin Water (r癸) month stem. This configuration brings the support of powerful leaders or guardians to any field in which he chooses to excel.

From the structure of the pillars, we can see that there are three Water signs, representing wealth, united as a team and likely to create a Follow Wealth system. The Dog (H戌) stands as a troublesome Sibling, thwarting his attempts to succeed. Fortunately, however, the Rabbit (t卯) is close enough to anchor it by pairing, preventing it from taking detrimental action. This helpful feature denotes a great problem solver, with the versatile ability to eliminate obstacles. Melnichenko succeeds in becoming a Follow Wealth type. He has three favorable elements: Water, Metal (which empowers Water), and Wood (which enfeebles the Self). His two harmful elements are Earth and Fire.

At the age of 21 in 1993, a Rooster year with Yin Water, he co-founded and chaired the MDM Bank; in 1997, at 25, an Ox (Metal) year, he bought out MDM Bank shares from his partners and became the sole shareholder. These events took place during his Snake period, which joined the Ox or Rooster to form a Metal team empowering his Water.

In 2000 (MW庚辰) at the age of 28, when the Metal Dragon joined his Rat to form a Water team, he co-founded the MDM Group comprising industrial assets of coal and minerals.

YEAR	AGE	LUCK CYCLE	KEY EVENTS
Prior to 1993	<21	Yin Wood, t乙	Graduated from Kolmogorov Physics and Mathematics School (FMSH-18), and the Plekhanov Russian University of Economics
1993-1997	21-25	Yin Wood to Snake, t-f乙-巳	Co-founded and chaired the MDM Bank. Studied Finance and Credit; bought out MDM Bank shares from his partners to become the sole shareholder
2000-2001	28-29	Snake, f巳	Co-founded the MDM Group comprising industrial assets of coal and minerals
2007	35	Horse, F午	Member of the Bureau of the Board of Directors of the Russian Union of Industrialists and Entrepreneurs
2015	43	Goat, d未	Ranked 137th in the *Forbes* World's Billionaires list (12th in Russia)

Ramona Rizzo and **Keisha Whitaker** are actresses from the United States.

Angie Hart is a rock singer from Australia.

10 LEONID MIKHELSON
B. AUGUST 11, 1955 (KASPIYSK, RUSSIA)

Leonid Mikhelson, is the chairman, CEO and major shareholder of the Russian gas company Novatek, Russia's second-largest natural gas producer. He is Chairman of the Board of Directors of ZAO SIBUR, and since April 2011 has served as Chairman at OJSC SIBUR Holding, a petrochemicals and gas processing company headquartered in Moscow with 26 production sites across Russia. Mikhelson is also the majority shareholder of SIBUR, and serves on the supervisory board of OAO Russian Regional Development Bank.

H	D	M	Y
n/a	T 甲	T 甲	t 乙
n/a	W 辰 華蓋	M 申	d 未 陽貴

BAZI SYSTEM • VARIABLE

	11	21	31	41	51
LUCK CYCLE	R 壬	m 辛	M 庚	e 己	E 戊
	F 午	f 巳	W 辰	t 卯	T 寅

The Self as Yang Wood, flanked by two more Wood signs, falls into a Sibling Rivalry configuration. The Siblings compete for financial resources, these being the Earth contained within the Dragon and the Goat. On the other hand, with a Goat on the year branch, the Self has the potential to become Dominant Wood upon the onset of a Rabbit or Pig. Mikhelson, therefore, has a Variable system.

In a Sibling Rivalry scenario, the Wood Self has two ways to win: it can either become Dominant Wood, or use Metal to rid itself of the other Siblings. Mikhelson, as a Yang Wood sitting upon a Dragon, is well anchored by Earth from the Dragon; apparently the stronger fighter, the Yang Wood Self is the ultimate victor of this configuration. However, additional Metal is needed as well as a good measure of hard work in order to succeed. As a Dominant Wood, Mikhelson could prosper easily. The bottom line is that the Self prospers either on Metal, or upon the formation of a Wood team.

Let us refer to his life events for verification. At 22 in the Snake year of 1977 (containing Metal) occurring in the midst of his Yin Metal period, Mikhelson's career took off as a pipeline engineer. At 32, in the Ox Metal year of 1985 during his Yang Metal period, he was promoted to chief engineer. Thereafter, over a long series of mostly Metal periods in his luck cycle, Mikhelson enjoyed a smooth upward sail.

During his Rabbit Wood period from 46 to 50, Mikhelson became Dominant Wood. He was entrusted to lead a holding company, amassing substantial wealth. As he entered the Tiger period, a Wood Trio of Dragon, Tiger and Rabbit took place in 2011 (mt 辛 卯) and he was promoted to Chairman of OJSC SIBUR Holding. By 2012, with the accumulation of additional good fortune from his new position, he had become a global-ranking billionaire.

YEAR	AGE	LUCK CYCLE	KEY EVENTS
1977	22	Yin Metal, m 辛	Graduated in Industrial Civil Engineering; foreman at a pipeline construction company in Siberia
1985-1994	30-39	Yang Metal to Dragon, M-W 庚-辰	Chief Engineer and General Director of a company renamed NOVA, after the dissolution of the Soviet Union
1994-2008	39-53	Yin Earth to Rabbit, e-t 己-卯	General Director of NOVA's holding company, Novafinivest, later known as NOVATEK
2011	56	Tiger, T 寅	Chairman at OJSC SIBUR Holding since April 2011
2012	57	Tiger, T 寅	On the *Forbes* list of billionaires

In stark contrast, **Sergei Mavrodi**, born on the same day in Moscow, gained notoriety as a fraudster and charlatan. His own recollections suggest that he had been highly skilled in mathematics and physics from an early age. Sources state that Mavrodi graduated in 1978 with a mathematics degree specializing in artificial intelligence from the Moscow State Institute of Electronics and Mathematics, becoming a computer programmer thereafter. He was also elected a deputy of the State Duma in 1994.

In the wake of declining support from his waning Yang Metal (M 庚) period in 1989, the Self fell prey to Sibling Rivalry. It was during this time that he established a pyramid scheme company, MMM, with two others.

On April 28, 2007, aged 51, he was sentenced to over four years in a penal colony for defrauding more than 10,000 investors out of an estimated 110 million rubles.

In the Pig year of 2007, while Mikhelson enjoyed Dominant Wood status at the helm of a leading corporation, Mavrodi was jailed for fraud. What can account for the stark differences in fate and fortune between two individuals born on the same date? After all, the onset of a Pig year should also have made Mavrodi Dominant Wood, enabling him to take full control of the Yang Earth, his financial assets. Sadly, it seems that Mavrodi had fallen too far under the sway of his Sibling Rivalry configuration, rendering Yang Earth the focus of intense competition. He failed to harness enough Wood flow to become Dominant. Of note is the fact that by operating a pyramid scheme, Mavrodi sought money for its own sake, with no real contribution to society in exchange; those with Sibling Rivalry systems are advised to avoid making money the main motivation of their endeavors, focusing instead on accomplishments. Let us take a look at how the two useful flows created differences between the lives of the two men.

Mikhelson was born and raised in Kaspiysk (latitude 42 degrees north), a warmer place than that of Mavrodi's native Moscow (latitude 56 degrees north), which would have been too cold to sustain the flow of Wood. As a strong Wood Self, Mikhelson will have harnessed this environmental support to inject more Wood flow into his system, making his later transition into Dominant Wood that much easier. In Mavrodi's case, the deprivation of such environmental support, compounded by a dearth of Wood in his own birth system, means that he was never furnished with the amount of Wood he needed in order to facilitate this transition.

The useful Metal flow from Mikhelson's studies in metal engineering was able to enrich his birth system as well as his transition into a Metal career thereafter. Focused Metal would have helped him lead big projects. Mavrodi, on the other hand, never worked in Metal fields, thereby failing to amass enough usable Metal energy. The nature of his various professions or ventures also varied greatly throughout his career. As a rolling stone, he remained trapped in a Sibling Rivalry system, struggling to survive, and vulnerable to losing battles and mischief. A good Bazi certainly makes life easier, but cannot account for the vagaries of personal choice and free will.

11 VLADIMIR POTANIN
B. JANUARY 3, 1961 (MOSCOW, RUSSIA)

Vladimir Potanin was born in Moscow to a high-ranking communist family. In 1983, he went to work for the Soviet Department of Trade, where his father had worked before him. He is the founder and owner of Interros Holding Company, and has been its president since 2008. He also owns a 30 per cent stake in Norilsk Nickel, and is one of the wealthiest men in Russia with a net worth of 15.3 billion dollars (April 2018, *Forbes*).

H	D	M	Y
n/a	F丙	E戊	M庚
n/a	M申 (戊庚壬)	R子	R子

BAZI SYSTEM · FOLLOW POWER

	11	21	31	41	51
LUCK CYCLE	M庚	m辛	R壬	r癸	T甲
	T寅	t卯	W辰	f巳	F午

The Self is Yang Fire, a symbol of the sun. Born in a rainy winter month of a watery year and on a wet day, the sun is fundamentally functionless. He has to surrender to the dominant flow of Water for provision and protection, becoming Follow Power. His beneficial elements are Water and Metal, whilst his challenging elements are Fire and Wood.

With mostly Metal and Water paving his luck cycle all the way through to the age of 51, he began succeeding exponentially from 30 years old. The powerful Water trio formed at the onset of his Dragon period, between the ages of 36 to 38, placed him in a politically and financially beneficial position, poised to reap huge profits. The Snake period created a Water merging from ages 46 to 50, conferring honors and recognition from prestigious clubs.

At 51, however, Potanin entered the Yang Wood period (T 甲), and a phase of rebellion began as the Wood flow empowered his Fire Self. In 2013 at the age of 52, shortly after entering Yang Wood, he initiated divorce proceedings against his then wife Natalia. As allegations of his extra-marital affair surfaced, Potanin paid a huge price, becoming estranged from his children as their family unit disintegrated.

YEAR	AGE	LUCK CYCLE	KEY EVENTS
1983	22	Yin Metal, m 辛	Graduated from Moscow State Institute of International Relations; worked for Ministry of Foreign trade
1991	30	Rabbit, t 卯	Created the private Interros company
1993	32	Yang Water, R 壬	President of United Export/Import Bank
1997	36	Dragon, W 辰	First Deputy Prime Minister of the Russian Federation
1998	37	Dragon, W 辰	President and Chairman of the Board of Directors of the Interros Company, owning 30% of Interros, and controlling Russian Nickel giant, Norilsk Nickel

YEAR	AGE	LUCK CYCLE	KEY EVENTS
2003	42	Yin Water, r癸	In charge of the National Council on Corporate Governance (NSKU), legislative regulations in Russia on ethical standards of corporation
2003-2007	43-47	Snake, f巳	Chairman of the board of a Russian art museum in 2003; member of the Public Chamber of Russia in 2005; Officer of the prestigious Order of Arts and Literature 2007
2013	52	Yang Wood, T甲	Divorced in December 2013

Álvaro Monteiro Magalhães is a football manager and former Portuguese footballer, who played as a left back. Álvaro represented Portugal at the 1986 World Cup and Euro 1984 during his Dragon period, a prime time in his life.

12 MIKHAIL PROKHOROV
B. MAY 3, 1965 (MOSCOW, RUSSIA)

Mikhail Prokhorov is the principal owner of Onexim Group, a private investment holding company. As one of Russia's leading industrialists, Prokhorov owns major stakes in multinational corporations in the precious metals sector.

In June 2011, at the age of 46, he resigned his corporate positions to enter politics, focusing his efforts on the establishment of a new political party in Russia, known as Civic Platform.

H	D	M	Y
n/a	f丁	M庚	t乙
n/a	f巳 (庚丙戊)	W辰 (癸戊乙)	f巳 (庚丙戊)

BAZI SYSTEM · VARIABLE

	19	29	39	49	59
LUCK CYCLE	E戊	f丁	F丙	t乙	T甲
	T寅	g丑	R子	r亥	H戌

The Self is Yin Fire. Born in an Earth month and surrounded by three more Earth elements (contained within the 巳辰巳 formation), he has a Follow Children system. As two of the Earths are found in the Snake (巳), which chiefly contains a strong Metal flow, he could easily form a Metal team with the onset of an Ox or Rooster. Figuratively speaking, this Metal flow becomes his Grandchild, keeping his provisions in an unbroken chain of supply - a great blessing.

This Metal team could also grant him Follow Wealth status, given that Metal is the wealth element of a Fire Self. The process could take place twice in every 12-day or 12-month cycle, or in any Rooster or Ox year. In other words, he could score during any Rooster or Ox day, month and year, as well as for a continuous five-year period during his own Rooster or Ox luck cycle.

Naturally, Prokhorov's good fortune is Metal-related. During his Ox period from the ages of 34 to 38, he became a Follow Wealth, strategically acquiring an international company for expansion and planning to separate from his partner to become fully independent.

There is another beneficial feature in his system. The Dragon in his month branch, when paired with a Tiger, brings a sudden surge of fortune. In the table below, we can see that from the ages of 24 to 28 during his Tiger period, Prokhorov landed critical positions with ease, connecting him with the partners he needed to build his fortune.

He welcomes Water as it controls the Fire, safeguarding his Follow status. A Water team could also be formed whenever a Rat or Monkey sets in, transforming him into Follow Power, and enjoying the good fortune this confers. Thus, the useful elements are Earth, Metal and Water, whilst Fire and Wood become his dreaded foes.

YEAR	AGE	LUCK CYCLE	KEY EVENTS
1989-1992	24-27	Tiger, 丁寅	Graduated from the Moscow Finance Institute; manager at the International Bank for Economic Cooperation
1992	27	Tiger, 丁寅	Partnered with Vladimir Potanin to run Interros
1993	28	Tiger, 丁寅	Chairman of the Board for Potanin's Onexim Bank

YEAR	AGE	LUCK CYCLE	KEY EVENTS
1995	30	Yin Fire, f巳	Interros purchased Norilsk Nickel, a mining/smelting company, becoming the world's largest producer of nickel and palladium
1996	31	Yin Fire, f巳	Appointed to the board of directors of Norilsk Nickel
2003	38	Ox, g丑	In charge of the acquisition of StillWater Mining, his first international venture
2007	42	Rat, R子	Prokhorov and Potanin bought Norilsk Nickel from workers for a fraction of their estimated market value. Prokhorov's share of the company was worth $7.5 billion when he departed
2011	46	Rat, R子	Resigned both positions to enter politics in June 2011
2014	49	Yin Wood, t乙	*Forbes* estimated his wealth at $10.9 billion

Robert Brydon Jones (Rob Brydon) is an English actor, comedian, singer and impressionist. He has enjoyed a long and fruitful professional career, the Rooster year of 2005 being one of his most productive, with three film releases and several notable TV and radio features under his belt. In 2013, a snake year, Brydon was awarded an MBE. The Metal effect is clearly reflected throughout.

John "Faxe" Jensen became the head coach of Danish club Fremad Amager after a successful soccer-playing career which spanned more than a decade.

Gary Mitchell is a Northern Irish playwright. By the 2000s (Metal and Water effects), he had become one of Northern Ireland's most lauded playwrights, earning various accolades for outstanding achievement in his field.

13 DMITRY RYBOLOVLEV
B. NOVEMBER 22, 1966 (PERM, RUSSIA)

Dmitry Rybolovlev is a cardiologist, businessman, investor, and philanthropist. Both of his parents were medical doctors. He derives his fortune from Uralkali, Russia's largest producer of potassium fertilizers, and sold his stake for 6.5 billion dollars in 2010. In 2015, year of the Yang Wood Goat, he was ranked 156th on *Forbes'* list of billionaires with a net worth of 8.5 billion dollars.

H	D	M	Y
n/a	t乙	e己	F丙
n/a	m酉	r亥 (甲 壬)	F午

BAZI SYSTEM · VARIABLE

	15	25	35	45	55
LUCK CYCLE	m辛	R壬	r癸	T甲	t乙
	g丑	T寅	t卯	W辰	f巳

This is a marvelous system. By strict definition, the Yin Wood Self, being born in a Pig month, should fall under the sway of Sibling Rivalry. A rare stroke of genius, however, transforms the chart into Follow Resource. The Yang Wood Sibling (T甲), hidden in the Pig (r亥), is being discreetly paired up by the Yin Earth above and, in the process, frees Yang Water (R壬) to support the Yin Wood Self. In Bazi code, this process is termed a *Secret Pairing* or *Underground Pairing*; it entitles the Self to surprising sources of fortune.

Being empowered by Metal from the Rooster, this Yang Water is a super strong provider and protector. The Pig, after all, is the foundation of his livelihood - for preservation of the Self, it has to stay intact. Such a functionally intelligent and elegantly-crafted Bazi produces a highly-sophisticated individual - sharp-witted, opportunistic, personable and visionary.

The Bazi also has the added boon of being a Variable system. As a Yin Wood Self, his Pig on the month branch could join with a Rabbit or Goat, creating a Wood alliance and creating a Dominant Wood Self. In 2007, a year taking place during his Rabbit period, both Uralkali and Belarusian Potash Company (BPC) benefited from the increasing price of potash, and had one of the most successful Russian IPOs ever on the London Stock Exchange. Riding on the Rabbit flow, he branched out to acquire another potash company.

Given such a scenario, we can deduce that Rybolovlev thrives on Water and Metal whilst dreading Earth. During the 15 years of Metal and Yang Water from the ages of 15 to 29, he enjoyed the conscientious and professional support of his parents, becoming a cardiologist and earning his first million from a medical company he co-founded with his father. In 2005, a Metal year taking place during his Yin Water period (r癸), Rybolovlev became the chief executive of the Belarusian Potash Company (BPC).

Since the Pig is his vital source of Water, keeping the Pig intact is the most crucial strategy. Since a Tiger pairs it up and a Snake clashes it away, both breaking up his resource supply, they are his worst enemies. Indeed, trouble began at the onset of his Tiger period during a Snake month (May 1996), when he was arrested and indicted for the contract killing of a former business partner. After a key witness recanted his testimony, Rybolovlev was released from prison 11 months later. These events perfectly illustrate the aforementioned scenario in which the mischievous Tiger tries to pair up with the Pig, while the Snake attempts to clash it away. The process broke up his Follow Resource status and he was punished as a consequence. He sold his shares in Uralkali for a large sum of money in exchange for freedom. For the next four years, he worked hard to reorganize his firm. Shortly before entering the Yin Water period, Rybolovlev was able to push the firm to a more productive and profitable level.

The Yang Wood on its own, however, puts him in a Sibling Rivalry configuration. Rybolovlev was 48 in 2014, a Yang Wood year occurring during his Yang Wood period, when he was fined by a Geneva court to pay his ex-wife 4.02 billion Swiss francs (4.8 billion dollars). However, as the Goat in the following year of 2015 (td乙未) made him Dominant Wood, Rybolovlev's lawyers successfully appealed the ruling and the settlement was vastly reduced to 564 million Swiss francs. What had started out as the most expensive divorce in history eventually became the most expensive divorce reduction in history - a most desirable turnaround for Rybolovlev in the game of cosmic flows.

YEAR	AGE	LUCK CYCLE	KEY EVENTS
1990	24	Ox, g丑	Graduated from Perm Medical Institute as cardiologist. Set up Magnetics, a company offering alternative medical treatment, and was paid with discount products; earned first million dollars from high profits on resale of products
1992-1994	26-28	Yang Water, R壬	Obtained Russian Ministry of Finance certificate entitling him to deal with securities; opened investment company; founded a bank; acquired shareholdings in many of Perm's industrial enterprises; joined their boards

YEAR	AGE	LUCK CYCLE	KEY EVENTS
1995	29	Yang Water, R壬	Sold most of his shareholdings, focussing on enterprises operating in the potash industry, in particular, Uralkali
1996-1997	30-31	Tiger, T寅	Arrested in May 1996; in prison for 11 months; sold his shares in Uralkali in exchange for his freedom
1998-2005	32-39	Yin Water, r癸	Reformed and increased productivity of Uralkali by 2.5x
2005-2007	39-41	Rabbit, t卯	Uralkali's IPO on the London Stock Exchange became one of the most successful Russian IPOs ever
2010-2011	44-45	Rabbit, t卯	Sold stake in Uralkali for $6.5 billion; bought potash producer, Silvinit, and formed one of the world's largest potash producers
May 2014 (TF甲午)	48	Yang Wood, T甲	Divorce made headlines when a Geneva court awarded his ex-wife a record settlement of $4.8 billion
2015 (td乙未)	49	Dragon, W辰	Settled a divorce with his ex-wife in a payout of 564 million Swiss francs, a huge reduction from the previous settlement

Michael Kenneth Williams is an American actor and dancer, raised in the Vandaveer housing projects of New York City. Despite an underprivileged background, and armed with a marvelous Bazi, he landed a long, productive, and successful acting career in film and television.

Richard Stanley is a South African film director and screenwriter. After a few changes of residency in South Africa and London, he works and lives in France, and is a descendant of famed explorer Henry Morton Stanley.

14 GENNADY TIMCHENKO
B. NOVEMBER 9, 1952 (GYUMRI, ARMENIA)

Gennady Timchenko owns Volga Group, investing in energy, transport and infrastructure assets. In 2001 he declared an income of 4.9 million euros, and in 2002 at the age of 50, moved to Switzerland, presumably due to its preferential tax treatment.

H	D	M	Y
n/a	e己	m辛	R壬
n/a	d未	r亥	W辰

BAZI SYSTEM · VARIABLE

	19	29	39	49	59
LUCK CYCLE	r癸	T甲	t乙	F丙	f丁
	g丑	T寅	t卯	W辰	f巳

The Self is moist Earth controlled by a Wood team of Pig and Goat, under powerful Water. He becomes a Follow Power, and a beautiful one at that. As the flow of Water is so pronounced, however, a Water team could also make him Follow Wealth. Furthermore, being a Yin Earth Goat Self, he is one of the Intelligent Six. He is intelligent, quick-witted, compromising, pleasing, and has the ability to achieve a phenomenal degree of success with ease.

His beneficial elements are Wood and Water, while Metal is the most detrimental. Overall, his optimum habitat should be humid and woody. Timchenko spent his childhood in Germany, which has a moderate climate, conducive to the thriving of trees. Later, he studied and built his career in Saint Petersburg, a riverside city with enough humidity to promote the beneficial flows of Wood and Water.

From the age of 10 and extending all the way to 50, Timchenko's luck cycle consisted of either Wood or Water, with the exception of Metal/Earth between the ages of 25 and 29, during which he worked as an entrance-level engineer for a plant specializing in the building of power generators. From the age of 30, bolstered by the onset of Yang Wood in his luck cycle, he seemed to be moving on a fast track upward, from senior engineer, to a deputy director, to a leader in Russia oil trading, and finally to the CEO of International Petroleum Products Oy (IPP).

The impact of the Rabbit period from the age of 44 was unparalleled, and saw Timchenko's income increase tenfold between the ages of 47 and 49. In 1997, aged 45, he collaborated with a fellow businessman on a global commodity trading company which would later become Gunvor. In 2014, Timchenko amassed a vast fortune by selling his stake to the other co-founder, which placed him firmly among the ranks of global billionaires.

His good fortune extended to the Yang Fire period which followed, when it eliminated the Yin Metal from his birth chart. The Yang Fire also brought him to Switzerland in 2002, a relatively warmer environment.

YEAR	AGE	LUCK CYCLE	KEY EVENTS
1977	25	Ox, g 丑	Worked as an engineer for the Izhorsky plant near St. Petersburg, building power generators
1982-1988	30-36	Yang Wood, T 甲	Senior engineer of the Ministry of Foreign Trade

YEAR	AGE	LUCK CYCLE	KEY EVENTS
1988	36	Tiger, T寅	Deputy Director of state-owned oil company; his teams set up some of the first export routes of oil products from the USSR to the West
1991	39	Yin Wood, t乙	Hired by a Finland-based company, Urals Finland Oy, specializing in routing Russian oil to Europe; also became a Finnish citizen
1995	43	Yin Wood, t乙	CEO of IPP OY (renamed International Petroleum Products Oy, IPP)
1997	45	Rabbit, t卯	Co-founded the global commodity trading company Gunvor with Swedish businessman Torbjörn Törnqvist. He sold Törnqvist his stake in March 2014, a day before the US sanctions
2007	55	Dragon, W辰	Founded the Volga Group (Volga Resources Group) private investment fund
2014	62	Yin Fire, f巳	Ranked 62nd on *Forbes'* billionaires list, with an estimated fortune of $15.3 billion

Sherrod Brown from Ohio, United States, is a graduate of Yale University, lecturer at Ohio State University, and a US Senator. The year 2007 was monumental for both Timchenko and Brown alike: Timchenko founded the Volga Group private investment fund, while Brown entered politics as a senator.

Jim Riggleman, born in New Jersey, United States, has enjoyed a long and successful sporting career as a baseball player, coach and manager.

John Megna was a film and stage actor, having majored in performing arts at Cornell University, New York. He had been an active performer from the age of six or seven years old. Tragically, he died of AIDS in his early forties while Timchenko was still riding on a tide of good fortune. Cosmic flow by itself cannot account for his early death in a period when his counterparts were prospering during good luck cycles.

15 VIKTOR VEKSELBERG
B. APRIL 14, 1957 (DROHOBYCH, UKRAINE)

Vekselberg is the president and owner of Renova Group, a large Russian conglomerate. He is close to the Moscow Kremlin, overseeing plans for the economic modernization of Russia. According to *Forbes*, his fortune was estimated at 13.6 billion dollars as of August 4, 2015, making him the fourth richest person in Russia.

As an art collector, Vekselberg is the owner of 15 Fabergé Eggs, the largest private collection of Fabergé Eggs in the world, valued for their significance to Russia's cultural heritage. In 2013, he opened a museum in Saint Petersburg to return the treasures to their homeland.

H	D	M	Y
n/a	F丙	T甲	f丁
n/a	W辰	W辰	m酉

BAZI SYSTEM • VARIABLE

	13	23	33	43	53
LUCK CYCLE	R壬	m辛	M庚	e己	E戊
	T寅	g丑	R子	r亥	H戌

This is a clear Variable type. As he was born in a powerful Earth month and the same powerful Earth day, he could easily fall into a Follow Children configuration with the onset of additional Earth. When the two Dragons are joined by a Rat or Monkey, however, they could also form a Water team, creating a Follow Power system. Thus, his beneficial flows are comprised of two conflicting elements: Earth and Water.

Metal reinforces the Water flow, while Wood and Fire disrupt his Follow status. With a Yang Wood and Yin Fire in his month and year pillars, he needs remedial support from external flows to enjoy this Follow status. Fortunately the luck cycles are all in his favor from the ages of 23 to 42. With the Metal continuing in unbroken succession until age 38, he was able to curtail the Wood and reinforce his beneficial Water flow, accumulating assets through the founding and merging of companies. At 39, huge profits were realized again as he entered the Rat period, co-founding and acquiring new companies.

Vekselberg finally consolidated all his assets into a new kingdom as a Follow Children type, aged 46, at the peak of his moist Earth (e己) period. This angel Yin Earth played a magic hand in the elimination of a key blockage - the Yang Wood (T甲) in his energy system.

Nevertheless, in 2009, aged 52 during the last leg of his Pig period (which contained the T甲), Vekselberg was caught on violations of securities law and fined 38 million dollars. The onset and continuation of Yang Wood for that five-year period had finally taken its toll. Still, he bounced back with Yang Earth at the age of 53, entering the global billionaires club in 2015.

YEAR	AGE	LUCK CYCLE	KEY EVENTS
1979	22	Tiger, T寅	Graduated from Moscow Transportation Engineering Institute; engineer and research manager at state-owned pump manufacturer
1988	31	Ox, g丑	Founded NPO Kovek
1990	33	Yang Metal, M庚	Co-founded Renova Group with classmate Leonard Blavatnik

YEAR	AGE	LUCK CYCLE	KEY EVENTS
1996	39	Rat, R子	Co-founded Siberian-Urals Aluminum Company, becoming world's top; owned portion of Tyumen Oil, Russia's major oil and gas company
1997-1998	40-41	Rat, R子	Secured controlling interest in Tyumen, becoming Chairman of the Board; integrated it and other assets under Renova Group
2003	46	Yin Earth, e己	Chairman of TNK-BP, a joint venture between partnership of some Russian business groups (AAR consortium), and British Petroleum
2009	52	Pig, r亥	Fined $38 million by Swiss authorities on violations of securities law
2015	58	Dog, H戌	4th richest person in Russia

Mikhail Pletnev, also Russian, is a renowned concert pianist, conductor and composer, such achievements clearly reflecting the Metal effects. Interestingly, his destiny was genetically determined - his parents were both musicians.

The Wood effect, which saw Vekselberg penalized at the age of 52, also hurt Pletnev, with the timing slightly off but close enough for comparison. In July 2010, a watery Goat month, Pletnev had barely stepped out from his detrimental Pig period at the age of 53 when he was arrested by Thai authorities in connection with allegations of child molestation. At this particular juncture, the Goat had seized upon the last vestiges of Wood from the passing Pig to forge a Wood team, breaking up his Follow status, and subjecting him to punishment and censure.

Nevertheless, the charges were dropped on September 28, 2010, and he resumed his career two months later. What is so special about this date? It was a powerful Metal day (mf辛巳) in the most powerful Metal month of the year - the Rooster. He was able to escape the charges because the Wood flow at this blurry transitional period between luck cycles was too fleeting to produce a lasting result; it was easily defeated by the advancing of powerful Metal. For Vekselberg, however, his unfortunate event took place firmly within the Pig period when Wood was in full charge; he had no way to escape penalty.

Johnny Rumley from North Carolina, United States, is an American race car driver who won twice in the Busch Series races in 1993 and 1995. He apparently benefited from the flow of Metal, given the car's composition as chiefly Metal in nature.

Bobbi Brown from Chicago, United States, is a makeup artist who founded Bobbi Brown Cosmetics and wrote several books on beauty. Cosmetics deal with skin which is classified as Metal.

§

ENERGY SYSTEM	Variable 13		Follow 3	
ENVIRONMENT	Freezing cold	Rich in Water and mineral resources	Focal point of economic and political opportunities	
AGE AT FIRM'S INCEPTION	<30 7	31-40 5	41-45 4	

USEFUL ELEMENTS	Metal	Water	Earth	Wood	Fire
	10	10	6	4	0

EDUCATION	Engineering	9
	Science	2
	Economics	3
	Medical	1
	International Trade	1

Fig. 8a: Summary of Russian Billionaires

At the completion of this chapter, let us sum up our key findings in figure 8a above.[4]

From the chart, we can see that not only do 13 of the 16 individuals have a Variable system, but more remarkably, that each Variable system includes at least one Follow configuration among its possibilities. What is more, they achieved their biggest successes when the Follow configuration came into play in their lives. The remaining three Bazis, which do not have a Variable system, fall entirely into the Follow category. In other words, every individual has at some point or other been under the sway of a Follow configuration. The outcome confirms a Bazi code, which holds that "the truly successful faithfully follow their provider."

Figuratively speaking, the "provider" can be interpreted as simply what it takes to succeed. How do these individuals adhere to the

---

4 Note that these 16 include the case study of Alisher Usmanov already discussed in Chapter Four (p.56). Numbers indicate billionaires involved per classification.

proverbial laws of success? To begin with, they are sharp enough to understand the unique advantages as well as the limitations of their habitat, yielding and adapting to it for survival. Russia is a cold country of dense Earth, rich in minerals, with the best resources concentrated in Moscow, a land of infinite opportunity. The most receptive will have realized that a sure path to prosperity lies in cultivating an aptitude for minerals and Earth. Tellingly, over half of our Russian billionaires studied engineering, with the rest in the technological or financial sectors. They flocked to Moscow to seize opportunities along the way, never losing sight of that magic provider, minerals. Over 90 per cent of the foregoing case studies worked or invested in resources connected with minerals, the lifeblood of Russia.

Interestingly, their career choices are complemented not only by their natural habitat, but also by compatible energy systems, that is, by a cosmic predisposition to achieve success. Indeed, this demonstrates the very workings of destiny itself - to have the right potential, to be in the right place and time, and finally, to make the right choice.

The great majority of our samples have Metal or Water as their useful elements; Earth, as a runner up, empowers Metal; the role of Wood is marginal, while Fire is pushed out of the picture entirely, given Russia's subarctic climate. We have no doubt that a large number of Russians are born into excellent systems which satisfy the Bazi codes of success and yet rely on Fire as their useful element. Unfortunately, the odds of Fire thriving in the climatic conditions of Russia are poor, and given the lack of environmental support, these individuals fail to rank among its billionaires.

One question remains: why have those with the duplicate Bazi systems of these billionaires led such vastly divergent lives? As the *I Ching* holds, it takes the interactions of Yin and Yang, the pairing yet opposite forces, to create and sustain good fortune. The *I Ching* sage, Shao Kangjie, asserted that, without the proper personal initiatives and dedication to develop it, even the best Bazi system could ultimately become a worthless one. It bears repeating that a favorable birth system needs to be complemented by the right choices of career, time and place. While the individuals in our sample all possess auspicious Bazi systems, they have also demonstrated a strong sense of destiny in all their dealings, pursuing it with unstinting dedication.

CHAPTER NINE

CONCLUSION

Our investigation sheds light on the reality of success by comparing identical birth data from several of the 21st century's prominent society and industry figures. The sample may be small in number and not as randomly selected as it could have been, yet results from the study have been dependably consistent. Readers are welcome to test our findings by conducting their own research, using the rest of the sample as a starting point.[1] Although we have examined only half of these 96 charts for the benefit of the current book, we have no doubt that further research outcomes would fall in line with those advanced here.

This book has been the culmination of many years of study into the mercurial nature of success. We have concerned ourselves particularly with the *quality* of this success, which exhibits great variety even among those who have been born with the same energy system. The analysis of duplicated birth composites is a new frontier in Bazi research and, we hope, one that adds crucial dialogue to the fundamental laws governing the spectrum of success. If the book is used and understood as intended, there should be ample opportunity for readers to build a rich reserve of metaphysical insight.

Let us sum up the findings. Firstly, an auspicious energy system forms the foundation of prosperity, this much is undisputed. What is particularly conducive to the flourishing of success, however, is the existence of a powerful and focused form of cosmic energy. These are

---

1 See Appendix.

precisely the parameters that escape our individual control. We are born into inequality, the result of finely-tuned cosmic calibrations, the nature of which falls beyond mortal comprehension.

Secondly, this focused energy is not uniform in its effects - where the same energy systems prevail, personal choice becomes the decisive factor, just as the *I Ching* preaches that an interaction of Yin and Yang is needed. The same energy interacting with different individuals, or to the same individual at different times, bears fruit of varying quality. From the life trajectories of our sampled individuals, we can see the breadth of these variations played out in real time.

What is it that influences one individual to make a particular choice when presented with the same set of resources as another? In the West, many of those with exceptional cosmic systems - typically those belonging to entertainers and sports personalities - owe a great deal of success to being able to follow in the footsteps of parents, siblings, or other trailblazing associates within the same orbit of influence. In Russia, many of our billionaires have single-mindedly applied themselves to the few opportunities afforded them, taking pains to earn the qualities needed to climb a rigidly-established social order,. Similarly, our modern Chinese billionaires have seized on new opportunities granted at the right time, even in the midst of hostile social and political conditions. Many others have been buoyed up with the flow, serendipitously finding themselves in the right place at the right time.

The idea of upgrading one's Bazi with good deeds, as discussed at the start of the book, is crucial, and brings us to our third important finding. Works proceeding from personal attributes such as dedication, integrity, having the right knowledge and attitude, as well as a desire to serve our fellow man, are certainly key ingredients. However, the mechanism underpinning cosmic inequality seems to involve far more than Shao's stipulated good works. Variables including inherited DNA and the impact of one's physical and socio-political environment are equally critical. Significant success is ultimately brought about by perfecting the interaction between human effort, and the flow and timing of one's cosmic topography. In other words, we seem to be faced with the insurmountable task of perfecting "luck".

While perfection may only come from the Almighty showering auspices on a chosen few, the average person can also go some distance to achieve great things, albeit perhaps in a less-than-perfect way. Deeds can be defined by their magnitude (impact), and varying grades of quality. The common man can undertake a good deed that matches his cosmic potential, launching it at the onset of the right flow.

As for the right place, not everyone has the ability to exercise that option. After all, the function of Bazi is not about precise predictions of a specific life event, even though many unfairly expect it to be just that; it is rather about understanding how individual flows work at a given juncture, and attuning to them properly in order to bring about the best case scenario. While the lucky one plays his hand with divine intuition, others have to learn the skills of attunement.

Finally, if we could wish our readers to come away from this book with one lesson in mind, it would be to realize the power of agency and personal accountability in the pursuit of metaphysical knowledge. There is no universal formula that can be applied to the entire spectrum of human endeavor. The impact of cosmic energy varies widely according to the individual, to which the stories contained within these pages provide ample testimony. Success of the non-fleeting kind is derived from careful planning. To know our energy is to understand how to go about enriching it, seizing upon the right flow for targeted action. It takes knowledge and skill to walk in the cosmic topography. When we pair the flow with correctness of action, time and place, the options we take will allow us to sail in harmony with the greater cosmic plan.

While the principles of Bazi may be accessible to all, the right interpretation is a reward and privilege, gained only through diligent observation and testing; there must be a symbiotic relationship between the metaphysician and his subject, rather than a blanket application of theory. A reading has to account for past actions as reliable indicators of future response to the same flows, and only through careful examination of a subject's case history can this be effectively determined.

We hope that these insights will give earnest students the impetus to examine their own Four Pillars, not as an ironclad and predetermined hand one is dealt, but as a fluid and evolving organism, that responds sensitively to external action, environment, and free will.

APPENDIX

The following is a list of the 48 additional samples used in the study, which are not discussed in this book, but which may form the basis of further research:

NAME	DATE OF BIRTH	BAZI TYPE
Sheldon Adelson	Aug 4, 1933	Follow Power
Steve Ballmer	Mar 24, 1956	Follow Wealth
Ramon Barba	Aug 31, 1939	Follow Children
Edward Bass	Sep 10, 1945	Follow Resource
Elliot Belgrave	Mar 16, 1931	Follow Wealth
Andris Bērziņš	Dec 10, 1944	Variable
Paul Biya	Feb 13, 1933	Follow Power
Sara Blakely	Feb 27, 1971	Strong Self (on Resource)
Sergey Brin	Aug 21, 1973	Variable
Tory Burch	Jun 17, 1966	Dominant

NAME	DATE OF BIRTH	BAZI TYPE
David Cameron	Oct 9, 1966	Dominant
Juan Carlos I	Jan 5, 1938	Follow Wealth
Steven Chu	Feb 28, 1948	Variable
Alpha Condé	Mar 4, 1938	Dominant
John Doerr	Jun 29, 1951	Follow Wealth
Larry Ellison	Aug 17, 1944	Variable
Rosalind Franklin	Jul 25, 1920	Variable
Sonia Gardner	Feb 16, 1962	Variable
Mamnoon Hussain	Dec 23, 1940	Follow Children
J. Hans D. Jensen	Jun 25, 1907	Follow Children
Steve Jobs	Feb 24, 1955	Follow Resource
Jerry Jones	Oct 13, 1942	Weak Self supported by Resource
Abdul Qadeer Khan	Apr 1, 1936	Dominant
Phil Knight	Feb 24, 1938	Follow Resource
Charles Koch	Nov 1, 1935	Variable

NAME	DATE OF BIRTH	BAZI TYPE
David Koch	May 3, 1940	Variable
Mario Molina	Mar 19, 1943	Follow Resource
Gordon Moore	Jan 3, 1929	Follow Wealth
Dustin Moskovitz	May 22, 1984	Follow Power
Rupert Murdoch	Mar 11, 1931	Follow Wealth
Barack Obama	Aug 4, 1961	Dominant
Stefan Persson	Oct 4, 1947	Variable
T. Boone Pickens	May 22, 1928	Follow Power
Rosen Plevneliev	May 14, 1964	Follow Power
Choummaly Sayasone	Mar 6, 1936	Follow Resource
Richard Scaife	Jul 3, 1932	Follow Wealth
Stephen Schwartzman	Feb 14, 1947	Variable Wood
Thomas Siebel	Nov 20, 1952	Variable
George Soros	Aug 12, 1930	Variable
Steven Spielberg	Dec 18, 1946	Follow Wealth

NAME	DATE OF BIRTH	BAZI TYPE
David Thomson	Jun 12, 1957	Variable
Lynn Tilton	Apr 22, 1959	Follow Wealth
Jim Walton	Jun 7, 1948	Variable
Ty Warner	Sep 3, 1944	Follow Children
Steve Wynn	Jan 27, 1942	Dominant
Tadashi Yanai	Feb 7, 1949	Dominant
Jerry Yang	Nov 6, 1968	Follow Resource
Miloš Zeman	Sep 28, 1944	Follow Power

A SELECTIVE BIOGRAPHY OF DR. LILY CHUNG
WITH BAZI ANALYSIS

Dr. Lily Chung began her journey into metaphysics in April 1964, when a brush with a blind fortune teller initially failed to convince her that she was soon to migrate overseas. She had a teaching post in a boys' high school at the time and, under the economic imperative of having to support her siblings after the death of their father, took to this news with a strong dose of scepticism.

Born and raised amid the traditions, symbolism and superstition that flourished in the collective psyche of mid-century Hong Kong, Chung was no stranger to the Chinese people's reliance on metaphysical help. As a country still recovering from the recent Japanese occupation and return to British sovereignty, this was a landscape of political unrest, where its wary population stood by a cultural heritage steeped in the familiarity and consolation of metaphysical lore.[1]

As a teacher and academic, having recently graduated from the Chinese University of Hong Kong with a degree in History and

---

1 All of these metaphysical schools, regardless of structure, function or approach, derive their codes and principles from one source, the *I Ching* (or *Book of Changes*), and most use the Four Pillars of Bazi - *Bazi* meaning Eight Characters - as the fundamental building blocks of their philosophy. A good metaphysician, irrespective of the school or lineage from which they hail, must, therefore, be proficient in *I Ching* codes, as well as well-versed in Bazi, its most popular branch of Chinese metaphysics. With no formal printing system or copyright law in ancient China, the *I Ching* and its derivative systems were codified and documented by hand, this written tradition being passed from teacher to chosen disciples across the ages. Teachers established themselves as masters, and had absolute authority on their choice of student, as well as what - and how much - knowledge to impart. The practice was chiefly the preserve of male intellectuals, female masters making up an insignificant demographic in the field. Nevertheless it provided fertile ground for the endless creation of masters of all walks of life. While some sought advice as a matter of routine maintenance, for many it was a last resort after every other option had been exhausted.

Geography, Chung kept a careful distance from this esoteric practice, which seemed to stretch the bounds of intellectual credibility. Yet, on the last day of class that following July, just as she was packing for summer recess, Chung recalls a colleague entering her office with a stack of US college bulletins, informing her that he was going to study in the United States next month, and that the year after would be her turn. "These colleges are wealthy and welcome foreign students," he said. "Try to apply for an assistantship. See you in America."

Sensing the hand of fate for the first time, the tidings of the blind master were thrown into sharp relief. "You will soon migrate overseas," he had told her. "A mentor will hold your hand to the destination. This move will be followed by ten years of great luck."

Emboldened by the revelation, Chung decided to take a risk and set the terms of her relocation to the United States. After calculating the total expenditure for her study, along with the share of financial support owed to her family in Hong Kong, she sent out applications to 20 American colleges that November, stipulating an allowance of at least 240 dollars a month to make the move viable. Her terms were met by Kent State University in Ohio, where she received an offer of an assistantship to begin in September 1965. A three-week voyage by sea then brought her to American shores, setting events in motion that would ultimately allow her to expand the reach of classical Chinese cosmology to an awaiting Western readership.

Chung's own journey into metaphysics, however, did not truly begin until 1986, a point at which her life had taken a deep downturn on all fronts. By this time, she had completed her doctoral study in Geography and was living in California, when a series of unfortunate events recalled to mind the prescience of the old blind master, and along with it, an intuitive sense that only true metaphysical insight could help her restore inner peace. Some time later, her brother arrived from Hong Kong on an impromptu visit with a copy of the Chinese Perpetual Calendar, and despite being otherwise unversed in Bazi methodology, proceeded to chart the birth composites for several members of the family. Though the exercise was carried out for amusement, Chung read this as a sign that the study of Bazi was firmly within the remit of common folk and not merely the preserve of masters whose knowledge had been handed down through lineage.

Chung's education began with several research trips to and from her homeland, procuring and poring over the ancient classical Bazi texts that, within a year, would enable her to unravel the good master's prediction. Let us examine Chung's chart to better understand his technique.

LILY CHUNG
B. JULY 3, 1937 (HONG KONG)

H	D	M	Y
T甲	m辛	F丙	f丁
F午	t卯	F午	g丑

LUCK CYCLE	21	31	41	51	61
	e己	M庚	m辛	R壬	r癸
	m酉	H戌	r亥	R子	g丑

1965 was the year of the Yin Wood Snake (tf乙 巳). Chung was going through the Rooster (m酉) luck cycle at the time. With the Ox (g丑) in her chart forming a perfect combination of Snake, Rooster and Ox (f巳/m酉/g丑), the Self transformed into Dominant Metal, able to dictate and set the terms of its own fate.

How does a perfect Metal trio equate to long-distance travel in this instance? Snake is Chung's Mobility star, or in Chinese, the *yima* (驛 馬), which can literally be translated as a posthorse on duty. Acting alone, this "horse" is ill-equipped for travel, unable to move very far at all; as part of a trio combination, however, the horse is connected to a rider and fully prepared for the long passage ahead, which more than likely involves journeying overseas. By definition, a powerful and beneficial trio combination represents a Nobleman forging a path towards great fortune, and for Chung, the move turned out to be very lucky indeed.

The most interesting discovery, however, was that she would succeed in spreading metaphysical knowledge through the written word. There are two indicators to support this.

Firstly, Chung's Scholar star, the Rat (R子) includes one of her Peach Blossoms (the Romance star). The potential of this configuration points to one's ability to produce several books of acclaim. Although there is no Rat in her birth composite, Chung's initial publication, *The Path to Good Fortune: The Meng*, was published during the Rat phase of her luck cycle. The success of this book, which has been well documented here, set her on the path to becoming a metaphysician.

Secondly, the year pillar (fg丁丑) contains the Ox, Chung's Yin Resource element, which is able to dissipate the pressing force of Yin Fire (the Yin Ruler) and prevent it from hurting the Self. Selves with this configuration tend to be able to shore up substantial savings throughout their lives. They also have the capacity to leave behind a considerable written legacy.

What are the forces at play which could drive an individual to such a zealous pursuit of metaphysics? To start with, the bearer must have a crystal clear Four Pillars birth composite, keenly reflecting the effects of changing cosmic flows and naturally confirming the codes of Bazi. For Chung, the unmuddied and focused energy of her chart set her on course for life.

Secondly, as a weak Self, Chung possesses a powerful Yin Resource in the Ox. It contains moist earth, the most crucial force, strategically poised to protect the Self from the ravaging effects of Fire. The presence of a powerful Yin Resource at work is often encountered in configurations which promote the nurture of renowned metaphysicians. The Self learns to seek help patiently and humbly. In addition, Chung has three of the 12 Yin-Yang Mismatch pillars in her birth composite. These troublesome pillars galvanize individuals to take action by constantly fielding and solving problems, both their own and those of others. Such Selves are compelled to seek solutions with an open mind, transcending ordinary means through metaphysical insight. Practically all good metaphysicians have one or more such pillars.

Next, the chart contains two Void signs of strong Fire, each comprising a Nobleman in the two Horses (F午). To be Void, in this sense, is to be clear of blockage, both mental or physical. In mental terms, it manifests as an intense clarity of thought and vision, a penetrating mind that is able to pierce the veil of illusion in order to seek the best course for action. Physically, it could signify empty pockets, or any situation - such as career instability - characterized by a lack of support, depending on the nature of the signs. Void signs may also produce feats of great fortune when clashed by or teamed up with other signs. Those possessing these signs have a tendency to make sudden discoveries or achieve great success while searching tirelessly for some form of remedy or relief.

Lastly, as a Yin Metal Self, we can see her Metaphysical stars at play in the collaboration of the Pig and Tiger. These do not exist in the birth composite, but are significant when we consider that Chung began to pursue her calling in 1986, a Tiger year occurring during her Pig luck cycle. She also signed a contract with her publisher for *The Path to Good Fortune* in 1995, a Pig year. During the Tiger luck cycle, Chung published five books in her native Chinese with two of the top publishers in Hong Kong. Three of these five were subsequently translated into English and published in the United States, from which one was translated into Russian, going on to become a Four Pillars bestseller in its own right.

Chung has been closely studying Chinese metaphysics for over 30 years, and her expertise encompasses not only Four Pillars energy analysis and the geomantic remedies of *feng shui*, but also extends to lesser-known *I Ching* divination systems such as the *He Luo Li Shu* (河洛理數). She is chiefly preoccupied with the question of cosmic inequality, devoting much of her research to understanding the source of the highs and lows of fortune peculiar to the human condition. Her motivations lie in helping others to live a more meaningful life by attuning themselves to the momentum of their own cosmic flow.

Chung has taught geography in colleges in Pennsylvania State, the Chinese University of Hong Kong, and the Baptist College of Hong Kong. As a teacher of metaphysics, she has taught at the City College of San Francisco and conducted workshops across Europe, Canada, California, and Hong Kong. She currently resides with family in San Francisco.

The Cosmic Geography of Success is Chung's 14th book and first collaboration with her student, Samantha Lam.

Other books by Dr. Lily Chung

- *The Path to Good Fortune: The Meng* (1997)
- *Easy Ways to Harmony* (1999)
- *Calendars for Feng Shui and Divination* (2000)
- *Succeed Naturally, the I Ching Way* (2008)
- *The Truth of Ups and Down: Cosmic Inequality* (2009)
- 長勝風水, 易經的特突破 (2011)
- 人人八字, 為自己找出成功的密碼 (2012)
- *Four Pillars of Destiny, Discover Your Code to Success* (2013)
- 實用易經, 新編河洛理數論命 (2014)
- 八字良緣 (2014)
- *Four Pillars of Destiny, Finding Your Life Partner* (2014)
- *Four Pillars of Destiny, Your Life Numbers & Hexagrams* (2015)
- 命運, 同命不同運 (2017)

26974007R00173

Made in the USA
San Bernardino, CA
24 February 2019